WIRED DIFFERENTLY
UNDERSTOOD TOGETHER

Creating neuroinclusive environments
at work and in life

Dr Joan van den Brink

Wired Differently, Understood Together

ISBN 978-1-915483-72-0

eISBN 978-1-915483-73-7

Published in 2026 by Right Book Press

Joan van den Brink masterfully cuts through the jargon around neuroinclusion by using a series of characters to present neurodiverse traits and experiences in different situations. This allows her to weave in a number of frameworks and models for creating more inclusive environments without leaving the reader feeling that they just have more things to remember. Accessible, clear and personable, as well as a joy to read.

– Dr Jan Peters MBE, coach and consultant

Joan van den Brink's rich coaching experience supporting neurodivergent individuals shines through every page, offering an honest and compassionate exploration of late diagnosis, love and belonging. What resonated most with me is her call for authentic neuroinclusion – creating spaces where neurodivergent people are not forced to shrink or fit in, but are empowered to thrive as their full selves. A powerful and much-needed contribution to the conversation on neurodiversity.

– Marcia Brissett-Bailey, multi-award-winning dyslexia advocate and author of *Black, Brilliant and Dyslexic*

With clarity and compassion, Joan van den Brink shares how *agape* – unconditional love rooted in acceptance, patience and grace – can transform relationships, systems and communities. As a neurotypical cisgender woman, this book has sparked my curiosity about the social identity cues related to neurodiversity that I may be missing. A timely and necessary read for anyone interested in understanding neurodivergence and its many faces.

– Sukari Pinnock Fitts, MSOD, PCC and co-founder, Fifth Domain Coaching

This thoughtful and encouraging book shows how we can better understand and engage with neurodivergent individuals, offering valuable insights into inclusion, workplace practice and self-advocacy. It is a genuine invitation to meet people as they are and create spaces where everyone can thrive.

– Nathan Whitbread, coach and founder of the
Neurodivergent Coach

Work can be one of the toughest places for neurodivergent people to show up as themselves, which leads to significant, negative impacts on both individuals and organisations. With this book, Joan van den Brink offers something that goes beyond the impossible quick fix: a framework for neuroinclusion that makes sense in the messy, unpredictable reality of the workplace. A powerful call to action to ensure that every person, regardless of neurotype, can feel valued as they are.

– Morgana Clementine, neurodivergent (AuDHD) author
and advocate

An exploration of the beauty and burden of being different in a world that demands sameness that offers a toolkit for connection. This book invites you to see, seize and share the untapped promise of neuroinclusion. If more people could truly grasp this potential and how to unlock it, our businesses – and our world – would be so much richer for it.

– Toby Moore, CTO and founder turned executive coach
to start-up leaders

A heartfelt exploration of neuroinclusion that offers a creative approach for coaches and coach supervisors seeking to deepen their awareness. Joan van den Brink encourages you to better understand the subtle dynamics that can either exclude or empower neurodivergent people by pausing and listening deeply, so that we can hold a more neuroinclusive space for everyone.

  – Will Medd, coach, supervisor and meditation teacher

Sometimes we are blind to things around us, not because our eyes are closed, but because no one has helped us understand what we are seeing. Joan van den Brink helps us explore our potential blind spots in regard to neurodiversity, providing stories, definitions, explanations and suggestions that will elevate your awareness of and aptitude for engaging with people in your life who differ from you in ways you may never fully understand.

  – Dan Newby, founder, Dignity Inc and author

If you're an HR professional or a business leader wanting to build a workplace where everyone is free to be themselves, this book is your secret weapon. It gives you a practical roadmap for not just understanding neurodiversity, but also making it a core part of your company's culture. Joan van den Brink's powerful and compassionate framework based on love, safety, social identity and dialogue is your answer to building spaces that are truly neuroinclusive.

  – Kathy de Gouviea-Smith, HR director, FMCG industry

Contents

Foreword

Joan and I met by way of my own writing, which focuses on my experience of being a late-diagnosed, multiply neurodivergent person. As well as a writer, I'm an educator, neuro-affirming trainer and a qualified coach who specialises in supporting neurodivergent folks.

I've worked in UK higher education for 15 years and have spent the past five years exploring what inclusive leadership looks like through my work leading and championing a majority-neurodivergent team of academics and careers professionals.

I've also experienced a lifetime of judgement, oppression and discrimination simply by showing up in the world as I am. So I know, first hand, how painful it is to walk through life out of sync with the majority of people, and how much extra effort I'm required to put in to succeed at things most take for granted.

Yet to build towards a future that is more welcoming of neurodivergent people and our differences, we need to move beyond relying on the resilience of the very people who are oppressed by current dominant norms. What is needed is wholesale, sustainable, systemic change. Yet change at this scale is only possible once we reach a critical mass of people actively engaged in this work. And this is where Joan – and this wonderful book – come in. Joan is an incredible ally to the neurodivergent community, sensitively seeking greater understanding of our experiences and looking at them through an intersectional lens.

I've lost count of the number of books I've read, written by my neurodivergent peers, which weave their own lived experiences into guides for living more authentic and nourishing lives. And these have been powerful narratives. Yet in writing sensitively and compassionately from the perspective of an ally, Joan is using her neurotypical privilege to amplify the needs of neurodivergent people and set out practical considerations for how we can all become neuroinclusive.

From the outset Joan describes how a single experience of receiving feedback that a training session she co-facilitated had not been neuroinclusive set her on the path to writing this book. Many neurodivergent people will know that our feedback and unexpected distress is frequently dismissed, so for this incident to be the catalyst for Joan to set forth on this journey speaks volumes of her own courage, compassion and wisdom. Indeed it is these Three Companions of courage, compassion and wisdom that provide the foundation for the powerful neuroinclusive framework Joan sets out in this book.

Joan has also been quick to recognise that the onus is on neurotypical people to make the overtures to create inclusive spaces. In setting out her framework so clearly and describing what the different elements look like in practice, she is equipping everyone with the tools to do so. The thought that this might be possible and that Joan, as someone who is not neurodivergent, might recognise the role neurotypical people must play in creating neuroinclusive environments gives me so much hope for the future – one in which we move beyond awareness towards truly embracing neurodevelopmental differences.

At a time when the wider rhetoric around neurodiversity too often centres around supposed over-diagnosis and efforts to 'cure' us of our differences, we need allies like Joan now more than ever. The scale of change that is needed is also not lost on Joan, and for this reason this book should act as a clarion call for us to come together and find the collective courage, compassion and wisdom required to create a world that is truly neuroinclusive.

Hannah Breslin, neuro-affirming coach, consultant and trainer

Prologue

I was feeling apprehensive. I was co-leading a workshop for a group of people who wanted to become coaches. This was day one of the programme and I was meeting the group for the first time. I felt a slight tension before the participants started to arrive, wondering how they would be, as individuals and as a group. *Would they come together? Would they gel with me? Would they recognise my expertise and authority for facilitating their learning?* All these thoughts passed through my mind as I checked the room set-up, got the materials ready and ran through the agenda... again.

I greeted my co-facilitator. We rehearsed the day and how we would engage with the group. My tension eased. 'It will be a great day,' I thought. 'We are experienced and know our stuff. We have carefully considered how we want to start so that we create a good learning environment. It's going to go well today.' I took three deep breaths and went out to the coffee station. I found some early comers and warmly greeted them. The day had started...

At 17:15, after the last participant had left for the day, I relaxed and let go of the leadership role I had held all day. I checked in with my co-facilitator to see how she was faring. We debriefed about the day and felt satisfied that we had attended to the group's needs as best we could. We had spent a lot of time in the morning working with the group to establish our learning agreement. This outlined our commitments to each other and how we would show up during those first two days. We dwelt on each point made so that the group had a shared understanding of the intent and meaning and how that translated to how we needed to behave. These included: participants speaking up if they were unsure what they should be doing or didn't understand a point; being patient with each other; taking care of their own needs, such as taking comfort breaks when required, getting themselves a drink. The participants had seemed interested and engaged during the day. Some members of the group spoke a lot, and others were quiet, particularly when the whole group were together. This felt like a routine start to a programme.

Day two progressed much like many others, with participants asking questions about the content, sharing their knowledge and experiences and taking part in the exercises. My colleague and I checked in with some of the quieter participants during the breaks and at lunchtime to see how they were doing. Nothing seemed amiss. Everyone appeared to be gaining new awareness, learning and insights.

I went home at the end of day two, pleased with how the first module had gone. Imagine my shock, a week or so later, at seeing that a complaint had been made about how that module had been run. I read the details with an increasing sense of shame. I had not realised that one of the participants, who is neurodivergent, had left feeling despair. I pride myself on my ability to show empathy and compassion for others and to create a safe space for them. I was horrified to learn that we had not done this for at least one person on the programme. I don't like negative situations hanging over me and wanted to put things right immediately. My inner critic had a field day. *How can you say that safety is your superpower when that participant didn't feel safe with you? You need to show courage and own up to your error at the next module. Use this as a teaching moment. You need to step down from delivering the rest of this programme because you've lost credibility.* And on and on.

Soon after, my co-facilitator and I were briefed by the head of faculty about the details of the complaint. I was relieved that most of the points related to the course design but still felt remorse that some of my behaviours had come across very differently to what I had intended.

I went on to facilitate the rest of the programme as planned, and to build trust and safety with the participant who had been so distraught. Receiving the complaint had been a tough and painful lesson that jolted me out of my complacency.

This experience propelled me on a journey to discover more about neurodiversity and how neurodivergence impacts the lives of those who identify as such. When I was studying for my inclusion coaching certificate, I had learnt about social identities and wanted to do more to foster inclusion. I made a pledge to bring coaching to individuals who would not ordinarily be able to access it. They could be disqualified for a variety of reasons, including belonging to marginalised communities. People who identify as neurodivergent are often ostracised by virtue of being different.

The two questions that I wanted to address were:

1. How can we create more inclusive spaces in which neurodivergent people feel safe to be themselves and celebrate who they are?
2. And how can we ensure that we all pay sufficient attention to this while not forgetting the needs of neurotypical people?

As a Nichiren Buddhist,[1] I strongly believe that we all have the innate qualities of courage, compassion and wisdom. I call these the Three Companions (van den Brink 2021). Our Three Companions enable us to be with others in a way that allows us to be a supportive presence when they are suffering and act in a way that helps to lessen their distress. I started an exploration to see how courage, compassion and wisdom could be used to create more neuroinclusive environments.

---

1 Nichiren Buddhism is a Japanese branch of Buddhism in the Mahāyāna tradition that is based on the teachings of the monk Nichiren Daishonin (1222–1282). The fundamental belief is that the Lotus Sutra contains the ultimate truth and that anyone can attain enlightenment in their lifetime through chanting 'Nam Myōhō Renge Kyō'. The emphasis of this practice is living fully in the present and doing the inner work to be the best we can be. We each have the power to positively impact our present and future through our thoughts, words and deeds. And by doing so we positively impact others and our environment. To learn more you can visit the following webpages: bbc.co.uk/religion/religions/buddhism/subdivisions/nichiren_1.shtml and en.wikipedia.org/wiki/Nichiren_Buddhism

Introduction

I'm fortunate that my work has enabled me to learn a lot about people. I'm passionate about creating intimate environments so that people thrive. To do this, I need to connect with them in ways that see them while at the same time honouring who I am. When I achieve this, I'm able to form profound connections in which they feel safe to reveal who they are and what experiences have contributed to this.

Over the past three years, as I've encountered individuals who have been late-diagnosed as neurodivergent, I have become more aware of their difficulties in being themselves in a society not designed for them. I was shocked to hear about the implicit and explicit negative messages from neurotypical people like me, who either didn't understand or didn't care to learn about the beauty that lies in who they are, as they are. Neurodivergent people are accustomed to being thought of as weird, not feeling valued for who they are, being told to think or act in a certain way, having difficulty in picking up on social cues, and neurotypical people trying to mould them into clones of themselves. The implication is that neurodivergent people need to study and adapt to how neurotypical people behave and interact. But this is a one-way street with few neurotypical people taking the time to ascertain how to best engage with neurodivergent individuals. The result is that neurodivergent people spend most of their time masking who they are so that they appear to fit in. This comes with a huge emotional, psychological and mental cost to them.

The more that I learnt about the experiences of neurodivergent people, the more strongly I felt compelled to act. I can be impatient and feel frustrated when I think that someone is 'going all over the place' when they are speaking. It takes all my reserves to stay with them. This is akin to the effort that neurodivergent people have to make to fit in with conventions. So, it is no surprise that they become exhausted, overwhelmed and burnt out. I have naively believed that I can connect with anyone in a way that allows them to be themselves and that they will trust and confide in me. It was a shock and rude awakening to realise that people still masked with me because what I was saying and doing made them feel that they couldn't be themselves. When I grasped this I wanted to make amends.

There are many great people who are experts in this field who are advocating for change for neurodivergent individuals. I wanted to add my voice to theirs in a way that is unique to me and, I hope, helpful and empowering. My voice is narrating another side to the story. This standpoint examines the relational dynamic that exists between neurodivergent and neurotypical people and how to create equality in that interplay. Let me illustrate. I am working with someone who has time agnosia. This means that they find it hard to determine how long a task will take. As a result, this individual has missed or been late for appointments. When they have been on time, it has been because they have made a supreme effort to put in place numerous reminders. I understand that and have empathy for this person and I wonder, if they are late, how long do I wait before abandoning the meeting? What will that do to their self-esteem? Is it legitimate to still end our meeting at the original time planned? Dear reader, you may feel that there are straightforward answers to these questions and maybe you're right. These are not so clear cut for me because my actions may inadvertently harm the individual in some way. As with all dilemmas, there is no definitive answer.

While this book may speak to many, I am primarily focused on how to foster neuroinclusion in organisations. This is because neurodivergent people have less choice and agency regarding how they demonstrate that they can contribute in valuable ways in the workplace than they do in other settings. They are expected to fit into the culture, observe norms, operate within rules and behave in specific ways. For example, I have heard countless examples of neurodivergent employees getting into trouble because they have spoken in a direct way or they have been vocal about something that seems unjust. Neurotypical people communicate in a way that is different to many neurodivergent individuals – there are social niceties to observe – but these are assumed and unspoken. When neurodivergent individuals do not comply, they are labelled as difficult, unsociable and uncaring. This can lead to neurodivergent people being wrong-footed numerous times a day. Having to constantly second-guess whether what they are saying and doing fits the social norms is demanding and leads to overwhelm and burnout over time. Outside work, neurodivergent people can choose who they hang out with, virtually or in person. Unsurprisingly, they gravitate towards other neurodivergent individuals who understand them without having to explain.

Working for an organisation means that you belong to some form of team, whether that is an intact team (a group of people reporting into the same person), a project team, a cross-functional team (comprising individuals from different functions within the organisation), a department, division, and so forth. The ideas in this book are designed to enable teams to be places in which everyone feels that they can fully be themselves. Each person is seen, heard and valued for who they are and what they contribute to the team.

I am hoping that if you are neurotypical, by reading this book you will increase your awareness of the types of experiences and journeys that your neurodivergent colleagues may have had and become more curious about what makes each person in an organisation special and unique. If you are neurodivergent, I wish for you to feel encouraged that there are allies who want to make the workplace somewhere that you can thrive and that you see that you play a significant part in making that happen.

If you are a leader of teams, whether you are neurodivergent or neurotypical, my aim is that you will ponder how you can create the conditions in which *everyone* in your teams can flourish and do their best work.

This is a complex topic that requires a momentous change in the attitudes and mindsets of millions of people. As a Buddhist, I believe that our environment reflects us and what we put into it. When we throw a stone into water, there is a ripple effect. I see this book as a small stone in the water that is life. I hope that the stories and messages that are contained here will move you to either strengthen or develop neuroinclusive practices. And by doing so, you touch and inspire others to do the same.

The Three Companions, courage, compassion and wisdom, can help us to see our trials as a normal part of life that enable us to grow as individuals. If we embrace them as learning opportunities and take the time to reflect on our experiences, we can build the resources and resilience to face future challenges with increasing equanimity.

As with my first book, *The Three Companions: Courage, Compassion & Wisdom*, I wanted to base this story on accounts that I heard first hand from people whose lives have been touched by neurodivergence. My aspiration was to uncover some keys to creating more inclusive spaces for neurodivergent *and* neurotypical people. I chose to speak with individuals who are neurodivergent or in relation with at least one person who is neurodivergent to hear about their experiences.

Being mindful of the ordeals that most neurodivergent people have had, I wanted to ensure that they felt in control of their narrative. I invited my interviewees to choose the stories that they wanted to share with me. I had no preconceived ideas and was curious about what was meaningful to them in their life experiences. My desire to learn about and from them meant that I gave them my respectful attention, listened deeply and responded to what they were saying.

The conversations that resulted were deeply moving and rich. Creating this space for them was important to them too. I was delighted to hear them use 'enjoyable', 'healing', 'revealing', 'cathartic' to describe how they felt at the end of the conversation. For me it was a privilege to witness these stories, which were told with such candour. It fortified my commitment to write this book. I feel compelled to use my voice to reveal the common humanity in our experiences with neurodivergence.

A note about language

I think it's useful for me to explain some of the less familiar terms that I am using and what they signify to me.

Neurotype

This is a term used to refer to classes of differently wired brains, ie neurocognitive ability. It describes the way that a person's brain processes sensory information and interacts with the environment. Neurotypes include autism, dyslexia, dyspraxia, ADHD, ADD and Tourette's syndrome.

Neurodivergent

Being neurodivergent is often described as having a mind that functions in ways which diverge significantly from the dominant societal standards of 'normal'. However, 'neuro' refers to nerves or the nervous system, so being neurodivergent is a whole-body experience. For example, rejection can be felt as intense physical pain in individuals who have rejection sensitivity dysphoria.

Neurodivergent individuals tend to have a 'spiky'[2] profile when it comes to their strengths and struggles when compared to neurotypical people. For example, they may be musically gifted, learning to play to a high standard quickly and being confident to perform on stage either solo or as part of a band, while simultaneously hating being in crowded spaces such as parties; or they may be able to solve complex problems with creative solutions but not able to structure their ideas and convey these either verbally or on paper in a way that makes sense to others.

Because I have spoken with individuals of various neurotypes, I want to think broadly about creating safe spaces for neurodivergent people in general. I have identified some common themes among these individuals that lead me to believe that this is a legitimate way of looking at this.

I am not saying that all neurodivergent people should be treated in the same way. Each person, neurotypical or neurodivergent, is unique and deserves to be treated as such. What I am advocating for is an approach that I believe will allow the neurotypical people among us to act in ways that allow neurodivergent individuals to feel respected and valued for who they are and not how the neurotypical world wants them to be. I single out neurotypical people here because neurodivergent people tend to 'get' each other. They are 'neurokin'. Neurokins share neurotypes and so tend to speak

---

2 A spiky profile is a term used to describe the strongly contrasting strengths and limitations in a neurodivergent individual's cognitive abilities. For example, high creative skills and low planning and organisation abilities. See geniuswithin.org/what-is-neurodiversity for a graphic representation of this.

the same language. There is no need to try to follow social niceties or apologise for information dumping about their special interest, for instance.

Neuroinclusion

What I mean by neuroinclusion is that we think and act in ways that are inclusive of all, ie how we think about and respond to each other in each moment. The trouble is that neurotypical and neurodivergent people often struggle to empathise with each other. There is often misunderstanding or misinterpretation about what one party is saying to the other because of their different experiences, ways of processing information and communication styles. This phenomenon is known as 'double empathy' (Milton 2018).

> **Neuroinclusion requires both neurodivergent and neurotypical people to be aware of the impact that we have on each other, curious rather than knowing, empathetic and compassionate instead of judgemental of each other.**

If we are being inclusive, when someone says something that, on the surface, seems weird, inappropriate or even hurtful, we pause to reflect on what might be behind their comment. When we arrange meetings we consider the needs of each person who will attend. This includes the space in which the meeting is being held, how the meeting is designed (see more later in Part 2, Bringing it all together; and Part 3, Generating neuroinclusion in work environments), finding various ways to share how information is conveyed and consumed.

Neuroinclusion requires both neurodivergent and neurotypical people to be aware of the impact that we have on each other, curious rather than knowing, empathetic and compassionate instead of judgemental of each other.

Structure of the book

I have interviewed 34 people specifically for this book. In addition, I have encountered neurodivergence in various aspects of my personal life and work. I have educated myself through courses, reading, listening to podcasts, radio programmes and watching documentaries.

I have structured the book into three parts. First, I chronicle the knowledge that I have gained through my conversations and experiences in **Part 1**. I build on this foundation to describe the building blocks for **Creating neuroinclusive spaces** in any context in **Part 2** and look at how to apply these to **Generating neuroinclusion in work environments** in **Part 3**.

My approach has been to create a fictional cast of characters who represent composites of the many stories that I have heard. Different aspects of neurodivergence are illustrated through these stories.

In Part 1, I illustrate various aspects of neurodivergence in **Tales of difference (Chapter 1)** by voicing the journeys and happenings of the main cast:

- Limbani, a mother's story
- Nathan, a father's story
- Xavier, son of Limbani and Nathan
- Phoebe, a partner's story
- Myles, partner to Phoebe
- Kala, a growing-up story
- Amelia, an HR story.

At first glance, you may be wondering why I am presenting these stories (Limbani, Nathan, Phoebe and Kala) because they are not wholly set in a workplace context. I believe that to create neuroinclusion you need to understand the entirety of someone's experience. Our home life, school encounters, relationships, friendships (or lack of) shape us consciously and unconsciously. It's important not to assume anything when engaging with others at work because neurodivergent people may be masking heavily to fit in and neurotypical people may have grown up or be living with neurodivergent people in their home.

Therefore, I have taken the time to elaborate the personal lives of these main characters so that you can relate to them as people and think about the possible happenings in people's lives and what they might be bringing to their work

Following on from these journeys, in **The common threads (Chapter 2)** I pull out recurrent themes across all the stories and journeys that I have written about with examples of how these might manifest.

Next, in Part 2, in **Creating neuroinclusive spaces (Chapter 3)**, I propose a framework that provides the foundation for building neuroinclusion. In this chapter, I explore the four elements that make up this framework in some detail to give you an appreciation of each.

Then, in **Bringing it all together (Chapter 4)**, I return to our cast and introduce a few more characters to show how we can foster neuroinclusion by looking at a series of events in which they gather to have a dialogue.

In Part 3, in **Generating neuroinclusion in work environments (Chapter 5)**, I provide some practical tips for developing neuroinclusion in organisations.

Part 1

Chapter 1

Tales of difference

Limbani's story

Limbani was reflecting on how her journey as a mother had unfolded. It had not been easy. Limbani had gone through the worries, doubts and anxieties that most new parents experience. She was proud that they had weathered some storms and come out stronger and wiser. Xavier, her son, had found his way in the world and was happy most of the time, but this had not always been the case.

Limbani first noticed that Xavier was developing differently to other children of his age when he was three-and-a-half. He was easily triggered when there were three or four people whom he did not know or there was a lot of noise. Then he would seem to turn into a different child, crying, shouting, throwing things, hurting himself, hitting her, etc. Initially she thought he was going through 'terrible twos' at a later age than most children. In fact, when she discussed this with her health visitor, she told her there was nothing to worry about and that he would grow out of it. But he didn't.

Things got worse when he started school. Limbani noticed that Sunday afternoons and evenings were particularly trying. Something seemingly trivial, like losing his ball in the bushes at the park, would trigger a disproportionate response, a complete meltdown. Xavier could be inconsolable for hours. She and her husband Nathan would have to draw on all their powers to remain calm and patient with him. On Sunday evenings they would struggle to get him to go to bed and sleep. On Monday mornings, Limbani had to grapple with him to get him dressed and in the car to go to school. While waiting on the edge of the school playground for the bell to sound that it was time to go in, Xavier would cling to her. She had to gently but firmly unpeel his hands from her. Just as quickly he reattached them until a member of staff came to take him into the classroom. This lasted for the first few weeks at school.

Parting like this was difficult and broke her heart. Limbani wondered if she was scarring him for life by sending him to school. Full-time education was a legal requirement, she knew that, and Limbani felt that this was best achieved in a school environment and yet it made him so unhappy. Limbani used to sit in the car and cry. At home, she would clear up the debris from the morning's tussle and then sit quietly with a cup of coffee as she attempted to switch gears and get into work mode.

At the end of the school day, most of the children emerged noisily from the school building full of exuberance. Xavier would seem subdued and couldn't wait to get away. If she was speaking to another parent he would tug at her sleeve and try to pull her away. So, she had little time to bond with other parents or make friends. She felt like a misfit in that community of parents. Limbani felt very much alone.

When Xavier first presented violent responses she had reacted by shouting and restraining him. She tried to discipline him by sending him to the 'naughty step', but he refused to sit quietly and either cried loudly or went into the living room to play. His protests got louder and more physical each time she took him back to the naughty step until she gave up, shattered. Often she was at her wits' end. When Limbani looked back on those times she felt ashamed of how she had behaved then but she didn't know any better. She didn't realise that he was neurodivergent.

Nathan worked long hours so the bulk of the childcare came down to her. She was happy to do it. This had been her choice. But motherhood was not what it had promised to be. She was often called into school by the headteacher for some misdemeanour Xavier had committed, such as shouting at another pupil, scratching, pinching. She could see that he was too afraid to say anything to her then. Later, when they were at home and calm, Limbani was able to ask Xavier about what happened. He had often been provoked in some way by other children until he reacted. The teachers seemed to miss these sneaky attacks on him and labelled Xavier as aggressive and out of control. Limbani tried to present his version of events but they wouldn't listen. The teachers put Xavier's behaviour down to a lack of discipline at home and implied that Limbani and Nathan were too lenient with him.

Limbani tried to instil stricter parental controls by insisting that he did his homework and went to bed at a reasonable time so that he could get up in the mornings – to no avail. Xavier became increasingly withdrawn at home and school. She could see him go into himself and he was showing signs of depression. He told her that he didn't want to live. This scared her. She wanted to protect him and keep him safe. She knew something was seriously wrong and felt ashamed. Limbani didn't want to ask other mums whether they experienced similar problems because she felt that would be admitting that she was a bad parent.

Limbani was desperate to know what to do. She had her heart in her mouth every time she let Xavier out of her sight, in case he would harm himself. Limbani was tired of not getting any relief or support from the professionals. She wondered what would happen if she decided to take Xavier out of school. She started researching his characteristics and behaviour patterns and often found herself in forums for parents of neurodivergent children. At first she didn't accept that Xavier might be neurodivergent. But the more she researched, the more she found herself in these forums. Limbani devoured the posts she found there and followed links to other resources, including podcasts and books. Limbani found her way to blogs and books written by mothers of autistic children.[3] She related to their experiences and was inspired by the way they had embraced their neurodivergent children. She read books on inclusive parenting that gave her ideas for how she and Nathan could parent Xavier in different ways.

One message that shone through from these numerous resources deeply impacted her. It was to trust her instincts. She was Xavier's mother; she knew him better than anybody. What did she think was the right thing to do? Xavier was now ten and still declining. Limbani knew that if she didn't act, something dreadful would happen. Armed with her knowledge and the encouragement of parents in one of the forums she belonged to, Limbani demanded that Xavier be assessed for neurodivergence. The head teacher was not convinced, but she realised that Xavier needed help to fit into the school environment. While the assessment process was

---

3 Such as the blogs by Carrie Cariello (carriecariello.com/mondays-blog-2) and Kate Swenson ('Finding Cooper's Voice: The secret world of autism', findingcoopersvoice.com).

long and involved, the child psychologist they were referred to was sensitive, kind and patient with them. The assessment was carried out at home where Xavier felt safe and Nathan and Limbani felt bolstered.

The outcome was that Xavier was diagnosed as autistic with ADHD. With this diagnosis, he was entitled to support. He was put on medication, which helped stabilise his moods and get him on an even keel. He was also assigned a learning support assistant (LSA) to provide one-to-one aid in his lessons. The LSA took time to bond with Xavier first, over several months. He showed him kindness and understanding. He told Xavier that he was aware that at times everything could become too much for him. He asked Xavier to let him know so that they could find a quiet space for Xavier to calm his senses.

This was a turning point for them as a family. Finally, Limbani felt relief. She wasn't a terrible mother after all! It had been challenging, even after diagnosis. Limbani understood what was behind Xavier's unhappiness, his feeling of overwhelm and his meltdowns. It made it easier to bear but did not provide her with a magic wand. Often she could predict which situations would be difficult for him and prepare him in advance. Sometimes she was caught off guard. This was particularly true when she could not control his environment – for example, in a public place where he did not understand the rules. Limbani learned to wait until after the heat of the moment had passed to sit down with Xavier and talk to him about what had happened and the impact that his behaviour had had on others. At times she wondered if this was doing any good because he seemed incapable of responding in any other way than how he did in the moment. Gradually, though, she saw that he did see when his behaviour upset her or others and was able to say sorry when he was calm again.

With the love and support that he received at school as well as at home, Xavier blossomed. Fast-forward to today. Xavier is 20 and in his final year at university. Limbani is proud of the young man he has become. He still finds it difficult to be organised and doesn't respond well to unplanned change but, for the most part, he is successful. He is aware that his energy can be depleted by trying to conform to societal requirements, which leads to meltdowns and burnout if he doesn't pay attention to warning signs. These are difficult for him to spot at the time, and this is when Limbani worries about him the most. She continues to have conversations about events so that they can both learn from them. Limbani is slowly letting go of the need to keep him safe and allowing him to develop his own strategies for navigating life.

Nathan's story

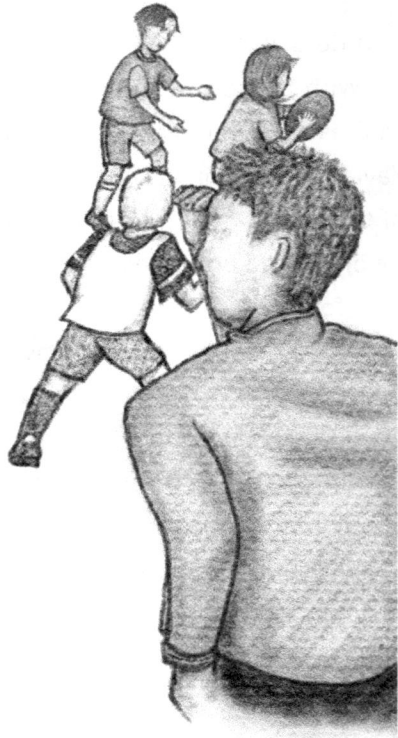

In the early years, Nathan had found Xavier's behaviour difficult. He wanted Xavier to be like other boys, in the thick of it like he'd been, playing football and rugby. When Xavier was seven, Nathan took him to the local rugby club, which was within walking distance of home. Xavier had watched from the sidelines but showed no interest in joining in. One of the coaches noticed him and asked him to play with the other boys. Nathan gave Xavier a gentle push to encourage him to go onto the pitch and join in.

Xavier stood a little apart from the others and tried to follow the instructions. Nathan could see that he was finding that difficult but was glad to see him making an effort. After 15 minutes of various drills, the coach put the boys into two teams to have a game for the final ten minutes. The coach blew his whistle and all the children ran towards the ball – all the children except Xavier, who was doing what he was told and staying out on the wing. He didn't try to get the ball and no one threw to him. He was happy to run around by himself. The game ended and Xavier came running up to Nathan. Nathan asked if he'd enjoyed it and Xavier said 'no'. It had been too noisy and he didn't like the way the kids ran up to each other to get the ball. He was glad they had left him alone. Nathan took Xavier to rugby a couple more times and finally realised that Xavier was never going to like it and join in. Nathan was so disappointed.

Xavier seemed to have sudden meltdowns. He and Limbani could not understand why he would fly into a rage out of the blue. Nathan would get angry and tell Xavier that he couldn't hit or kick him. He would hold Xavier so that he couldn't move. After several minutes of his wriggling to get free, Xavier would quieten. Nathan worked long hours and was often away from home, so mostly it was Limbani who was left to deal with Xavier. After a while, Xavier stopped being violent towards Nathan but continued to show less restraint when it came to Limbani. They were called into the school on several occasions about Xavier's behaviour but because Nathan travelled for his work, he often wasn't able to go to the meetings with Limbani. They knew something was wrong but had no idea what it was.

Nathan came from a big family and was close to his parents, two brothers and sister. Before Xavier was born they used to go to his parents for Sunday lunch and he was used to calling in every week for a chat. He and Limbani had attended various family functions such as birthdays, weddings, christenings and Christmas. While Nathan had felt some social anxiety, he generally enjoyed these gatherings. Now, however, they hardly went out as a family. Increasingly Nathan found he couldn't relax because Xavier would either withdraw and go and hide in a room by himself or get so distraught that they would have to leave early. They rarely had friends over or went out because they couldn't leave Xavier with a babysitter. Nathan felt embarrassed that his son wasn't like his nephews and resentful that his social life had become non-existent.

One day, when he was at his parents' house, his mother remarked that she saw some similarities between Xavier's behaviour and how Nathan had been as a child. Nathan bristled at this remark and demanded to know what she meant. His mother explained that as a child he had struggled in some social situations. He preferred to play alongside other children rather than with them. He hadn't understood why he was required to share his toys with someone else who wouldn't take care of them in the same way that he did. The big difference was that Nathan enjoyed playing sports and was quite good at them, so he was selected for the school teams. This also meant that he had made friends, although only one or two of these had become close and were people with whom he felt truly at ease.

Nathan thought about what his mother had said and started to observe Xavier more carefully. He recognised some similarities between the two of them. Xavier needed structure and routine. When this was disrupted, Xavier would often become anxious or have a meltdown. Nathan didn't like change either. He had learned to plan and prepare for his work trips. If he was going somewhere that he hadn't been before he would get anxious. He would ask many questions about where he was going, who he would be meeting, what he would be doing. If at all possible he would rehearse the route he needed to take so that he knew what to expect. Fortunately, he worked in a small team and they tended to go out in pairs. He knew his colleagues well, which helped him to stay calm. He hadn't made that connection with Xavier's meltdowns when they surprised him with trips or visitors.

Limbani and Nathan talked a lot about their worries and fears for Xavier and how they might help him. When Nathan shared with Limbani what his mother had said, and he had noticed, Limbani was thoughtful. She did some research to see if she could find some answers as to what was going on. When she told him that she thought Xavier might be neurodivergent, Nathan was shocked. That couldn't be possible. Yes, he had anger management issues, but surely he would grow out of them. Limbani and Nathan spoke for hours. Nathan wasn't sure about getting Xavier assessed. He would be labelled and that would disadvantage him. But he could see that Xavier was withdrawing more and more into himself. He spent most of his time in his room. Xavier had put a big sign up saying 'Do Not Enter' and would get physical if he or Limbani went in when he was playing games on his computer.

Limbani persuaded Nathan that having an assessment would be good for Xavier because then he could get the support he needed. When they went through the assessment for Xavier, he and Limbani each had to complete a detailed questionnaire that covered questions about their childhoods, experiences and information about life with Xavier. As he considered his responses to the questions, Nathan recalled how he had felt as a child and young adult. There were incidents he had forgotten about that came to the fore. Nathan noticed more similarities between how he had felt growing up and how life was for Xavier.

When Xavier was diagnosed as being autistic with ADHD, Nathan wondered if he was also autistic. But it didn't entirely make sense because he had played sports and liked socialising, which went against the stereotypical view of autistic people. When he paused to think about this, Nathan realised that he only liked socialising with his close family and friends. When the social circle got wider than that, Nathan became uncomfortable. He didn't know what to say or do and was stiff and awkward.

After the diagnosis, Nathan saw a change in Xavier over time. With the support of his LSA, Xavier was able to do well at school. Nathan learnt to better support Xavier, particularly through his meltdowns. He stopped getting angry and reacting in the heat of the moment and started talking to Xavier when time had passed and they were both calm. While their relationship was challenging at times, they had found some ease in each other's company. Occasionally they would do things together, which they both found enjoyable. Nathan became proud of Xavier rather than disappointed in him now that he better understood him and saw how he coped with life's demands.

Xavier's assessment was a turning point for Nathan as well. Nathan gained more self-awareness about why he would get angry when he felt out of control of situations or changes were introduced to his plans without warning or time to adjust. Nathan's new-found knowledge was only the first step in understanding himself. Nathan started to reflect on and talk about his experiences, particularly with Limbani. Sometimes this was hard because he often didn't know what he was feeling and why. When he was growing up, Nathan's parents hadn't encouraged talk of feelings, so Nathan had learnt to 'get on with it' irrespective of how he felt. He couldn't see the point in interminable talking. So, he got irritated when Limbani wanted to talk endlessly, it seemed to him, about her feelings as a mother and wife. He was learning how to give her enough time to process various situations in relation to Xavier and him so that she could recover her equanimity after a difficult event had occurred.

Phoebe's story

Phoebe had met Myles through work eight years ago. They worked for different offices in a large organisation and had met at one of the annual events. They had quickly hit it off and arranged to have dinner whenever work brought Phoebe to HQ, where Myles worked. Two years after meeting, Phoebe seized an opportunity to take a bigger role and transfer to the main office. Myles and Phoebe spent more time together and their friendship burgeoned into a romantic relationship.

Neither of them were in the first flush of youth, both having been in committed relationships before, so they wasted no time in moving in together.

Phoebe was attracted to his quirky nature and Myles's depth of knowledge on many subjects extending from philosophy to music to cars to sport. They would talk for hours and Myles would often follow up by buying her books to further her knowledge, showing her films, taking her on outings, etc. She found this charming. Wanting to please him she devoured the books so she could converse more. Myles's passion was music. She was fascinated that they heard music differently. For her music was a blended sound of all the tracks that she didn't think about. Myles, on the other hand, broke music down into each distinct part and analysed each one. He taught her how to listen so that she could distinguish the different instruments and voices. She found this endearing at first, but as time passed, she felt that he imposed his interest on her rather than tuning in to her level of curiosity.

Characteristics that Phoebe had initially thought of as adorable started to irk her. Myles would become consumed with a topic and spend all his spare time on it. He would research the subject to such a degree that he would often fall into rabbit holes of articles, research papers, interviews, blogs, etc. For example, one time he fantasised about becoming a stand-up comedian and spent all his spare hours studying acts and shows. Another time, he was taken with the notion of using telemetry to create a different automobile insurance model. When he was with her, he would talk to her endlessly about what he had learnt and the latest iteration of his ideas.

He showed no interest in her or what she wanted to do at these times. He would forget to eat or go to the bathroom, simply because he wasn't aware that he needed to. Initially, Phoebe found this strange. How could he not realise he needed to go to the bathroom? Surely, everyone knew how they felt at any time. She would go into his study when she hadn't seen him for two or three hours to ask how he was and if he would like to join her for lunch (or dinner). When he was in this flow state, he would either not hear her or mumble that he was fine without taking his eyes off what he was doing.

Myles had told her that he was autistic but she was sceptical because he was often the life and soul of the party. He loved to hold court and tell fantastical stories. He was great at entertaining others. This didn't fit with her stereotypical view of autistic people.

She was often surprised at how he reacted to things. For example, he could suddenly get angry about what seemed to her to be insignificant items, such as not putting the knives in a certain order on the knife block. He could not sleep if there was the sound of a ticking clock somewhere in the house and hated the sound of birdsong. What shocked her the most was that he could be charming to house guests and later say unkind things about them. As a result, Phoebe started adjusting her behaviours to fit in with his needs, not because he asked her to, but because she loved him and wanted to make his life as comfortable as she could. So, she always put the knives back in the right order and took the batteries out of ticking clocks. He relied on her to take care of their travel arrangements when they went away. He didn't like going to parties, nightclubs, concerts, the cinema or anywhere that would involve crowds, so she curtailed these activities, even though she loved to do them.

They started to argue about their differences – him not spending enough time with her, his tendency to start things but not finish them, her making too much noise, wanting to socialise, etc. At times he could be obstinate and impervious to how she was feeling. Phoebe couldn't understand how he could change from being attentive and caring to so lacking in empathy. She was baffled and found it upsetting. Fortunately, she had a calm temperament and didn't rise when he became grumpy. She wondered why some things mattered to him in this way and how she could improve the situation between them.

Myles had told her that he was autistic but she was sceptical because he was often the life and soul of the party. He loved to hold court and tell fantastical stories. He was great at entertaining others. This didn't fit with her stereotypical view of autistic people. When Phoebe asked him why he said he was autistic, he pointed to his auditory sensitivity and told her he could remember every car registration plate on the street. She didn't doubt this because he seemed to have extraordinary skills. However, she couldn't see how he could be autistic. Little did she know how narrow her viewpoint was. Phoebe didn't think any more about this conversation and would later realise that she was denying an essential part of his identity.

One evening she had gone out for dinner with some colleagues. They got on well together but rarely had the opportunity to relax and get to know each other. The conversation turned to relationship difficulties as one person had recently separated from her partner. Another colleague described some incidents that Phoebe could relate to as they were similar to her own experiences with Myles. Phoebe was intrigued by a throwaway comment that her colleague made about her husband's neurodivergence. When the general conversation had moved on, Phoebe quietly asked her colleague about how she had experienced his neurodivergence. As Phoebe later reflected on various incidents with Myles it dawned on her that maybe she had been wrong to dismiss his assertion that he was autistic.

Phoebe started to read about autism. One phrase that she came across repeatedly stuck with her: 'Once you've met one autistic person, you've met one autistic person.' This meant that autism manifests in a myriad of ways, so you can't claim to know what constitutes autism based on a few people you've met. Phoebe learnt that her view of autism had been influenced by what she saw portrayed in film and TV programmes rather than reality.

Phoebe's interest was piqued and she devoured information about neurodivergence more generally. She realised that she knew very little about the various neurotypes, and what she did believe were the stereotypes, such as dyslexia means having difficulty with reading and spelling words. She discovered that being dyslexic could mean being creative, spotting patterns and solving problems others can't.

It could also involve getting easily distracted, being confident when speaking but having difficulty expressing those same thoughts in writing. She was astounded to learn that dyslexic people could become mute, something she only associated with autistic people.

Phoebe could see that it was not only autism that manifested differently but neurodivergence in general. She realised that to fully understand Myles she had to let go of her view that autistic people rocked back and forth, made strange noises and were difficult to communicate with. She determined to suspend her pre-judgement of Myles and discover who he really was.

She began to see Myles in a different light – his hyper-focus on his interests, his deep knowledge about some topics, his intellectual prowess. His provocations, for instance not liking to be in crowds or where there was a lot of noise, also made more sense. Phoebe initiated conversations with Myles about what life was like for him. Now she was open to hearing about the discomfort he felt in some circumstances and what he struggled with. She uncovered that Myles had studied how neurotypical people behaved and developed some pre-planned scripts for how to act in various social situations. This explained how he could be charming in certain settings and rude about others when alone. Phoebe felt embarrassed that she had been so harsh and critical of Myles and apologised. She realised that his brain was wired differently; his spiky profile meant that there were things that he was brilliant at and activities where he needed support.

They started to explore how they might help each other

to bring out the best in their relationship. He asked Phoebe to remind him to eat during the day so that he could sustain his energy levels and not feel simultaneously elated and depleted after a long day. Phoebe agreed that when she was home, she would bring him drinks and small bites during the day and encourage him to take breaks. Phoebe requested that he asked her when would be a good time to share his latest passion with her instead of downloading and talking at her for long periods of time whenever he was excited about a topic.

Gradually, they found a better way of being together. This did not mean that everything was miraculously OK – it wasn't. Sometimes, she wished that he didn't rely on her so much and that he could take responsibility for some aspects of his life himself. When she felt this way, she was reminded of something a friend had once said to her: 'It's because you can.'

Kala's story

Kala had been labelled 'the weird kid' very early on. She didn't fit in at school. The other kids made fun of her, the way she spoke, dressed, her awkwardness. Everything about her was wrong. She was clumsy and often bumped into furniture, doors, trees, apparatus in the playground. She found it difficult to walk in a straight line and felt self-conscious walking anywhere. Because of this she either scurried out of the classroom before the other kids had realised it was breaktime or, more usually, she hung back until everyone else had left. Movement and hand-to-eye coordination were hard so activities that required this were excruciating for her – dance, gymnastics, arts and crafts.

She tried not to draw attention to herself during class and quietly did her work. Fortunately, she was strong academically, so was seen as a model pupil by her teachers. Kala found it hard to make friends because group interactions were overwhelming to her, so she kept to herself and was often alone. However, she was befriended by another girl in her class who didn't fit into the mainstream. Esther was more confident than Kala and looked out for Kala when the other kids teased or were unkind to her. The two girls soon became close friends. They were often to be found together in class and during the breaks. They developed their own code of communicating with each other and each found comfort in the other.

The time came to change schools. Kala and Esther were going to the same high school, but the school administrators decided to put them in different classes. Kala found the loss of her friend particularly distressing because moving to high school was bewildering and chaotic. In primary school all their lessons had been taught by the same teacher and they stayed in the same room. At high school they started the day in their forms and then had to switch rooms depending on what lessons they had each day. The lesson groups were based on ability and comprised a mix of pupils from different forms, so she would be with different people for different subjects. While Kala and Esther met after school and at weekends, during the day Kala had to fend for herself. Kala found this unsettling. She dreaded hearing the buzzer that sounded the end of lesson and a five-minute transition time to move to a different classroom. The halls and stairs filled with pupils hurrying along to get to their rooms before the buzzer sounded the start of the next lesson. She didn't like all the noise and bodies brushing past her or moving her along.

Kala became anxious during class and couldn't concentrate. She wasn't taking in any information because she was so fixated on safely getting to her next class. Where she had once been a star pupil, she was now failing. Her mother was concerned at this change in Kala and spoke with her form tutor. The form tutor reassured her that some students took a while to adjust to the high school environment and that Kala would soon settle in and go back to performing well. Instead of becoming used to this busy environment, Kala turned in on herself. She had felt enormous pride in her academic prowess. It was an important aspect of her identity. So losing this status had a big impact on her. She loved reading fantasy books and withdrew into this world. During breaks she could be found with her head in a book, either sitting in the classroom or on a bench in the playground. She read and re-read *The Chronicles of Narnia* by C S Lewis and books by J R R Tolkien. Kala became obsessed with *anime* and spent hours on her computer at home binge-watching episodes as she'd lose herself in the fantastical worlds. She knew every little detail of the characters, who was connected to whom, the powers that each character possessed, their idiosyncrasies and so forth.

Her mother was worried that Kala was not adjusting well and asked the form tutor what assistance might be available for Kala. There was a special educational needs coordinator (SENCO) at the school, so the form tutor arranged for the two of them to meet. The SENCO was empathetic and kind. She listened carefully to Kala's mother and gently spoke with Kala to hear what it was like for her. From her experience she suspected that Kala was neurodivergent and this was driving her difficulties with high school. Kala and her parents met with an educational psychologist who conducted the assessment. She was formally diagnosed as autistic with anxiety and depression. The psychologist supported and guided them on learning approaches that would help Kala to feel more at ease and able to learn. This included adjusting her timetable so that she had fewer transitions to make each day and could stay in a smaller, more constant group. This entailed spending part of each day quietly working on a computer in the library, which also constituted a place where she felt at ease. When she felt anxious or overwhelmed, Kala could go to the library where the quiet calmed her nerves. Kala was put under the care of a mental health professional who provided therapy to help her work through her emotions.

This assistance was monumental in enabling Kala to survive school and excel in her chosen subjects of maths, physics, chemistry and computer science. Kala did well in her exams. She wanted to go to university and made a careful review of the various options before narrowing down the choice to five. She arranged private visits to view the campuses and facilities and to meet the teams in the disability support offices. She discovered that several universities ran programmes to help students manage the transition from school to university and decided to sign up for one. The summer programme was daunting but the set-up catered specifically for neurodivergent students and she found that she enjoyed it. She made friends with other young people on the summer course, which was reassuring since she would know a few people when she started university.

While Kala had made friends during the summer camp, she found that they were in different classes and scattered over the campus, so it wasn't easy to meet them in person once they started at uni properly. However, the summer camp had given Kala confidence that she could make new friends and this enabled her to look for people who had similar interests as her. She joined the *anime* club and soon was meeting other people who were as passionate about *anime* as she was. She enjoyed discussing the intricacies of the characters and plot twists in the films. Most of the people in the club were neurodivergent like her. They were her tribe. They got her. She didn't have to explain when she felt 'othered' by lecturers, tutors or her peers. She could withdraw into herself when her reserves were low and they understood. And she could talk for hours about her latest interest without feeling she was over-sharing or talking too much. She felt most safe when she was with them and most able to be herself. When she was in other settings, Kala felt the pressure to conform and masked so that she wouldn't be thought of as weird.

Four years at university flew by and Kala graduated with a good degree in data science. She had become more confident in herself with the support of her friends. In her third year she became president of the *anime* club, which boosted her ability to interact socially. While she still found it hard, she became a good mimic of others and got by reasonably well. She was able to engage socially with others, although it cost her a lot of energy to do so. Others would see her having a good time and didn't see her collapsing in bed as soon as she got home.

The next transition for her was moving to the world of work. Kala became anxious about this phase as she didn't know what kind of job she wanted, how to apply for it or how to prepare for interviews. She turned to the Disability Support Service on campus for guidance. She was matched with a counsellor who helped her to write her CV, make job applications and prepare for interviews. Because Kala better understood her needs she was able to request information about each stage of the recruitment process, including the format of each interaction (online, in person, etc), whom she would meet and the interview questions. This was vital because Kala sometimes froze when she was asked questions she wasn't expecting, even when it was on a subject she knew well. Having this information allowed Kala to prepare and rehearse, which increased her confidence.

Kala entered some student competitions and was successful in two of these. These both led to invitations to interview with potential employers. Her preparation allowed her to shine in these interviews. After a few rounds with different companies and individuals she was offered and accepted a job in a technology company that provided digital solutions for organisations. What she found particularly appealing was the fact that the team worked virtually and met in person only twice a year. She was excited to begin this new phase in her life.

Amelia's story

Amelia worked in HR for a technology company that provided digital solutions for organisations. She had joined the company ten years ago as a specialist working in learning and development. She worked in a central team of experts designing and running various training programmes for staff. These ranged from providing guidance on how to use collaboration tools, for example, Teams, SharePoint, Slack, Trello and Miro, to navigating HR systems employed by the company, including Workday, HR information systems and learning platforms.

She had trained as an instructional designer and assigned to projects to design learning solutions for different parts of the organisation. In the early days she had been nervous to take on these assignments because they were new to her and there were many unknowns. She had doubted her ability to fully understand the needs and had felt exposed. She was afraid that she would not be able to answer questions posed by the senior leaders and they would think she was stupid and not know what she was doing. However, she was fortunate enough to have a wonderful line manager who gently pushed her out of her comfort zone but was always there to guide her.

Amelia had succeeded, and with each success she had grown in confidence. She moved from learning and development to join the talent management team, which looked after a pool of people across the company who were seen as showing potential to develop into the future leaders of the company. In this team she gained experience in how to think more holistically about the job requirements of key roles and map typical and non-traditional career routes that individuals could take to obtain the necessary learning experiences to be successful in these roles. She worked on several projects to partner with external organisations to develop state-of-the-art programmes that encompassed the latest thinking on various aspects of leadership.

Amelia was strong in engaging with people from around the organisation to understand their roles, background, challenges and objectives, marry these to the business strategy and design programmes that fulfilled the business need. And she enjoyed it. So, it had been a logical step for her to move three years ago to one of the biggest divisions within the company as their HR business partner. She worked alongside the leadership team to address the people issues that they faced. She led an initiative to redefine the culture and organisational values required to raise the performance bar of the division. A key aspect of this task was to embrace a centrally mandated focus on diversity, equity and inclusion. This included the establishment of employee resource groups (ERGs)[4] that focused on the needs of underrepresented or marginalised groups. Amelia

---

4 Employee resource groups (ERGs) are employee-led networks that are organised around common interests, affinities or some aspect of identity such as gender, race, colour, disability, sexual orientation. The purpose of these groups is to provide a safe space for members and foster a sense of belonging and to advocate for the needs of members. They are also a business resource if used wisely since leaders can learn from them about their experiences, how to build relationships and connections with people with similar interests or backgrounds in the community, test products and services and so on.

was part of the central team that spearheaded this effort across the organisation.

During the past three years in her current role, Amelia had gained an increasing awareness of neurodiversity. There were several programmes on TV in which celebrities described their experiences of either being neurodivergent or having children who were neurodivergent, or featured stories of autistic people to show how their minds worked.[5]

There was a plethora of podcasts, radio programmes and books about different aspects of neurodiversity and neurodivergence. It had become a hot topic.

Amelia became interested in this topic and went on several courses to learn more about it. On one level she was amazed at her ignorance and on another not surprised. She dealt with many HR issues of individuals not fitting in, unable to conform to certain ways of doing things, being seen as difficult or uncommunicative. As an HR professional, Amelia knew that there was often a hidden story that the individual was not ready to share. Over the years she had gained a reputation for building trust with these individuals who did not seem to fit the culture. She found creative solutions that enabled them to find roles within the organisation where they could work effectively.

However, she had not always been successful and now she was starting to realise why. There was a reasonable

---

5 For example, *Inside our Autistic Minds*, with Chris Packham, BBC 2, 2023; Paddy and Christine McGuinness, *Our Family and Autism*, BBC 1, 2022; *The Autism Podcast*, London Autism Group Charity; *That ADHD Story*, BBC Sounds, 2023.

chance that the individuals for whom she could not find a tenable solution were being forced to occupy a standard box. They were expected to have skills across a wide range of abilities such as communication, planning and team working as well as the technical skills that they needed for their job. She suspected that many of the people that she had been unable to support were neurodivergent, but of course she didn't know for certain. She hadn't understood that they had a spikier profile of abilities than the typical person – ie that they could be brilliant at some things, for instance, creativity, spotting patterns, visualisations, deep expertise in their chosen field – but potentially needed bolstering in areas such as planning and organising their work, time agnosia, delivering to deadlines, and understanding social and political cues.

She wanted to learn directly from the neurodivergent people in her organisation and was aware that this was a sensitive topic because there was a lot of stigma associated with it. Amelia took advantage of the colleagues who came to her with requests for accommodations at work to find out more about them, how their minds worked and what they needed from the organisation. She soon realised that being classified as a neurotype – for instance, ADHD – did not mean that everyone presented the same way or even that they could function at the same level from day to day. She also learnt from one neurodivergent colleague that it was taxing answering Amelia's questions. Constantly having to talk about her neurodivergent experience cost this colleague significant emotional energy that she found exhausting and frustrating because it led to little change in the organisation. Amelia wondered how she could learn more about the specific and unique needs of individuals in her division without taxing her neurodivergent colleagues.

One of the biggest challenges she faced was aiding managers in obtaining the results that they needed for the business while being responsive to the needs of their neurodivergent team members. While organisations are legally required to provide reasonable accommodations, some of the managers she encountered only paid lip service to this. This worried Amelia. She wanted to find a way to educate them about neurodiversity and neurodivergence so that they understood that this was a genuine difference in neurology and not someone wilfully being difficult. She wanted to create an ERG focused on neurodiversity, which she was willing to sponsor; however, this was proving to be problematic. Some managers supported her proposal, including a peer on the division's leadership team; however, neurodivergent people themselves were reluctant to sign up because they didn't want to be labelled and seen negatively.

Amelia decided to start small with a group of neurodivergent individuals who were not afraid to be visible in the organisation. She secured sponsorship from one of her peers on the leadership team who, it transpired, had a dyslexic daughter. Through his advocacy and her persuasive skills, Amelia was able to bring together a small group of people who were interested in the topic to start thinking about how they could adopt more neuroinclusive practices in the workplace. The group comprised neurotypical and neurodivergent individuals. They created an intranet site where they posted articles, videos and podcasts about neurodiversity and neurodivergence. The articles and videos were uploaded by members of the group to share their stories of triumphs and failures, what helped and hindered them. Slowly more people saw that the way the ERG was organised and run allowed people to participate as publicly as they wanted to. Some people joined sessions hosted by the ERG openly while others participated anonymously. They learnt that the purpose was to create a safe space for them to connect with others who had similar experiences or who wanted to be their allies and that it was not stigmatising.

One of the areas that the ERG tackled early was the HR approach to recruitment. They examined every stage of the process, from the screening of CVs to the way they conducted interviews. They implemented practices such as rewarding ERG members for referring neurodivergent people that they knew for open positions and providing detailed information about the interview process in advance. The latter included a short bio of the individuals that the candidate would be seeing plus a video so that they knew what they looked and sounded like. Amelia's team also asked what the candidate's specific needs were for the meeting and checked what the best approach was to hold the interview – in person, virtual, online meeting, phone call, etc – and a virtual tour of the building that the interview would be held in, if it was an in-person interview.

This approach was still in the pilot phase and Amelia was already seeing that this new style was resulting in an increase in the number of neurodivergent applicants and their success in landing roles in the organisation. A recent triumph was the recruitment of Kala, who was a fresh graduate in data science. Individuals with good degrees in this field were in high demand and there was a lot of competition in the market to secure them. Through the ERG, Amelia had reached out to universities to find ways outside the traditional graduate recruitment platforms. With the help of the recruiting manager, she had run a student competition at some universities to find individuals who had the technical skills they needed. Kala's entry was among a few that had stood out for her ability to spot hidden patterns among the data and formulate questions the answers to which could generate insights, leading to interesting opportunities. Kala was invited to interview at the company. Amelia immediately picked up Kala's anxieties about the recruitment process and was glad that their new approach seemed to address Kala's needs. Amelia was able to guide Kala to respond to the questions posed and share her knowledge confidently. As a result, Kala shone and was offered the position. Amelia was delighted when she heard that Kala had accepted and was looking forward to onboarding her to the organisation, providing the accommodations that Kala had requested and hopefully welcoming her to the Neurodiversity ERG as well!

In her endeavours to improve HR processes, Amelia encountered some stumbling blocks. For instance, some neurodivergent people did not know what they needed either prior to starting work with the organisation, being in their role or embarking on a new one. She tried to comprehend this and felt frustrated that some individuals could not express their requirements. This made it harder to put the right support in place. It took Amelia some time to realise that her efforts to help were also putting stress on some neurodivergent people who wanted to please her by responding to her questions even when they weren't sure what to say.

After the first flush of success, the excitement in ERG wore off and their momentum stalled. Amelia noticed that the energy levels and engagement by some of the neurodivergent members was waning. She was puzzled by this and asked her sponsor what he thought was the problem. He shared what he had learnt from his daughter and other parents of neurodivergent children. He explained that often neurodivergent people felt shame that they struggled with seemingly straightforward tasks, such as finding their way to a new location because their working memory is poor.[6] So they often hid their difficulties from even those closest to them. It cost a lot of emotional energy for the neurodivergent members of the ERG to educate the rest of the group about their experiences. Amelia had heard this before but felt that as she was making some changes, this did not apply to the ERG. She was annoyed at herself for not considering this in her eagerness to make the ERG a success.

Amelia was discovering more and more the complexities of fostering a neuroinclusive workplace. She felt out of her depth and decided to look for some external expertise to help guide her efforts and the work of the ERG.

---

6 Working memory is the ability to hold short-term (temporary) information in the mind while using that information to accomplish a task – for example, recalling a telephone number.

We will meet these characters again in Chapter 4, Bringing it all together, when they meet as a group with some new characters to engage in a series of gatherings that bring to life the elements I believe are vital to engendering neuroinclusion.

Chapter 2

The common threads

Do any of these stories resonate with you, either as a neurodivergent person or in your experiences with a particular person you have encountered? How well did you respond in the situations that you found yourself? What new perspective do you have from reading these stories rather than being in the thick of things?

Each of these stories could be parallel scenes in a TV programme about neurodivergence, where the scenes switch between the main protagonists and what happens to them. The audience gets drawn in as they observe different lives and the honest accounts of the joys and challenges faced day to day. Being exposed to these different cameos allows us to identify some common threads that are woven into each story. Let me pull each thread for you.

We are all the same, aren't we?

We each believe that we are experiencing life in the same way as others – the way we think, process information, sense our environment – until something makes us aware that this is not the case. This was true for me until a poignant conversation with a colleague opened my eyes. This event occurred more than 15 years ago and still stands out as a pivotal moment in my diversity and inclusion journey.

I prided myself on seeing the world as colourless and not thinking that I would be treated differently because of my skin colour. I have dark brown skin and short, curly salt-and-pepper hair. My mother instilled in me confidence and self-belief. Although I was often in a minority of one, I felt at ease and equal to my white peers. The moment I am referring to took place on the first evening of a two-day leadership development programme for healthcare leaders from ethnic minorities in the UK. I was co-facilitating with a lady from Pakistan. We were talking about how we each viewed the world. I declared that I did not think about my colour in my interactions with others. I will never forget how she responded: 'I see everything through my colour.' Wow! That sentence blew me away and shifted my mindset in a significant way. I went from dismissing colour as irrelevant to valuing the beauty that comes with being from a different culture or ethnicity.

> **We each believe that we are experiencing life in the same way as others – the way we think, process information, sense our environment – until something makes us aware that this is not the case.**

Nathan did not consider that he was different from others until he observed Xavier's struggles at school. Then he started to realise that his neurological processing was not the same as most people. This was also true of some of the fathers I spoke to in my interviews; I heard many stories where the narrator was not aware that there might be some difference. For example, one neurodivergent person told me that they had trouble with their coordination but thought that they were clumsy. They later discovered that they had dyspraxia, which affects movement. Another person struggled with anxiety but thought everyone did, so did not speak up. It was only when their mental health deteriorated significantly and they were given medical care that they realised that this was not normal.

Not fitting in

In each of the stories there was a realisation by the main character that they or their loved one were different from the mainstream. Limbani, Nathan, Phoebe and Kala noticed differences and quirks that were not easily explained by people developing at different rates, or seeing the world from a distinct philosophical or academic viewpoint, for example. Kala was seen as different by her fellow pupils and she felt it too. Only Esther befriended her at junior school. The other kids thought she was weird. Nathan desperately wanted Xavier to be a typical boy who played sport and joined in the rough and tumble, but he didn't want to. Phoebe was troubled by Myles's obsessions to the exclusion of other things and the detriment of his health.

Neurodivergent children are often considered weird, annoying, frustrating, difficult, lazy etc. They don't conform to societal norms and are ostracised in some way. They receive countless messages that their feelings and needs are unimportant. That they are wrong and need to conform. A common theme I heard was that neurodivergent people couldn't tolerate perceived injustice, particularly those who were autistic, and spoke out or acted to right this even though they knew that would get them into trouble.

There were instances where there was an expectation by parents of how the child was supposed to behave and no allowance was made or recognition given to what the child wanted. For example, being expected to attend family events and be sociable, or being groomed to fit into societal norms at school.

For most of the characters I have written, they had a few friends with whom they felt able to be themselves and not 'othered'. This was also true in real life. Many of the neurodivergent people I spoke with gravitated to individuals who understood them, and, as it turned out, they were most likely to also be neurodivergent.

Some individuals didn't realise that their way of being was atypical until much later in life. For neurodivergent parents this insight came from observing the struggles of their children (as we saw with Limbani and Nathan). For others it was from the prevalence of people talking and writing about neurodivergence and seeing that they had some traits which indicated that they might belong to this group. Individuals noticed that their partner's hobbies were all consuming (like Phoebe did). There was an intensity to these that felt extraordinary. And social interactions were not easy.

In each of the stories, there was a dawning realisation either by the person themselves or the person who was in relationship with them that they were different in their neurological processing abilities from social norms. For instance, Phoebe realising that Myles's interests went beyond what was considered normal. He got lost in his quest for information about his latest pursuit to the exclusion of other things.

Seeking to understand

Since they constantly get negative messages that their behaviour is unacceptable, neurodivergent people often mask who they are so that they do not stick out. They want to be liked, accepted and belong, as we all do. Over time the drain on energy involved in masking leads to overwhelm, dysregulation and burnout. I was amazed at how many of the people I spoke with were experiencing burnout.

Some symptoms of neurodivergent burnout include chronic exhaustion that does not improve with rest, loss of skills and ability to perform daily tasks, and increased sensitivity to sensory stimulation. In addition to long-term stress at work, neurodivergent people experience additional factors due to masking and having to constantly adapt to neurotypical expectations. Neurodivergent burnout can vary in duration from a few days to several months. Several of the people I spoke with were pushing through their burnout even though they had reduced functioning. Some of my interviewees told me that they experienced multiple episodes of burnout in a relatively short period of time. Recovery depends on the severity of the burnout, the individual's neurotype and their ability to access the assistance they need.

In some of the stories, the difference becomes magnified over time as the neurodivergent person struggles with aspects of life that make it hard for them to function in the way that is expected of them. Xavier and Kala both struggled in the school environment. They both became overwhelmed in noisy and chaotic contexts and needed to find quiet, calm spaces when they became emotionally dysregulated. Myles became angry when the order that he needed was disrupted.

Everyone is unique so some of the people I learned about in my conversations were able to recover sufficiently from their dysregulation without external intervention. One story that stands out is a person who became angry when there was a change to the holiday plans that she and her three friends had made. Another person, who was a friend of one of her friends whom she didn't know, was invited along. The storyteller froze this person out and didn't speak to her for the entire trip. It was many years later that she understood that the reason for this rudeness was her feeling a lack of control.

I heard many tales of the toll that not fitting in took on people, particularly on their mental health. It is not uncommon for neurodivergent people to have anxiety and depression. For parents of young children, this is particularly distressing. Not surprisingly, they are desperate to find out what is the cause of their deep unhappiness. Some mothers described these awful times and their fears for their children with such courage and fortitude. They fought to keep their children alive. They put their children's needs first rather than feel they had to conform to the rules to improve their child's mental health and wellbeing. Oftentimes that meant keeping them at home but also insisting on finding answers that would help them to obtain better support for their children.

All is revealed

Parents often knew that something was not right but were fobbed off by the professionals who should have been able to spot the signs better than the parents, particularly teachers. They wanted answers so that they could make life better for their children. The omnipresence of search engines meant that information was at their fingertips. They conducted their own research into symptoms to piece together the various fragments of the puzzle. Armed with knowledge, they could make a stronger case for diagnosis.

A similar dawning came for neurodivergent adults. They wanted to comprehend why they were unable to perform 'simple' tasks such as plan and organise their day or struggled to complete duties on time. I heard from an individual that he would walk into a room at home to do something and get distracted and start something else, so he rarely finished tasks. And yet, for some things to do with his work he was totally focused.

Reaching for a diagnosis only happened when the individual was ready or they felt there was a good reason to get one. Rationales for this included being on the verge of losing their job, knowing that it could help their neurodivergent child, after seeing their traits mirrored by them or to gain insight into themselves.

The real work begins

In all the stories I heard, getting a diagnosis provided relief as now there was an explanation for the difficulties neurodivergent people encountered in fitting in. They were not stupid or being difficult; their brains and bodies worked differently. This was the start of a new phase of self-discovery and understanding themselves. Some late-diagnosed neurodivergent people experienced grief for what their life could have been. On occasion they felt anger or incredulity that their neurodivergence had been missed by those closest to them. They wondered about how they might have developed differently if they had had the support they needed when they were growing up, entering the workforce and so on.

Knowing that they were neurodivergent didn't make everything wondrously OK. Many parents still struggled with getting the support that they needed for their neurodivergent children. The lucky few were able to access appropriate care. Their children were met with kindness and compassion. When the children displayed challenging behaviour, the school authorities tried to work with the parents to find a solution that was acceptable to all sides rather than punish the child. For some parents, the support was limited and difficult to access. For example, needing to send their child to a special school in a different neighbourhood and only for a few hours per day for a limited length of time. Funding for special education needs was revoked, which meant that bespoke support was withdrawn, and so on.

Neurodivergent adults knew that their brains and bodies

were wired differently but that awareness did not remove their social awkwardness, challenges in fitting in, problems processing information or sensory overload. Some days and situations required heavy masking or took a lot of energy – for example, participating in a training event with unfamiliar people. On these days, the neurodivergent person may have been cognisant of what was happening to them but unable to prevent the dysregulation from occurring and still required a few days to recover afterwards.

Learning what the diagnosis meant in reality came next. This is because, while there are some common characteristics, neurodivergence manifests differently in each person. For example, stomach issues are a symptom that many autistic people experience. Wanting to be in control and struggling with surprises was another. Their minds being busy all the time is a trait that many people with ADHD have. Someone told me it was like having a swarm of angry bees inside their brain the whole time. Individuals diagnosed as autistic with ADHD (AuDHD) often feel that the traits of the two neurotypes are in conflict. For example, wanting to have a routine and predictability (autism) but finding it difficult to stick to one (ADHD). Wanting novelty and change (ADHD) and becoming anxious when navigating change (autism). Having anxiety, depression and burnouts from trying to fit into a world not designed for them was prevalent in all types of neurodivergence. Being inquisitive and developing expertise in their special interests, thinking differently and bringing a different perspective, creativity, having a strong sense of justice and pattern recognition were some of the traits that made them extraordinary.

For parents of neurodivergent children, having a diagnosis meant not only greater appreciation for what their child was going through but also access to support and medication. For some that support meant the difference between survival and going under or off the rails. Some children and their parents did not want to be seen as different by having extra support at school and found their own coping strategies.

Knowing what each individual required was an ongoing quest of self-discovery as children became young adults and late-diagnosed adults learnt more about their neurotype.

A rich tapestry

For me, each person's tale can be likened to a panel in a tapestry that depicts part of the overall story of neurodivergence. While each person's life is distinct, the overall picture for neurodivergent individuals is one of inequity, and for many, oppression. Neurodivergent people are in the disadvantaged minority in society. Some societies and many neurotypical people do not acknowledge or are ignorant of this form of difference. Not all the people I spoke with had a feeling of safety in some part of their life, past or present. In some of the conversations I heard about, a child had been constantly on alert, fight or flight response primed at all times. They didn't have a nurturing environment at home. They were penalised for being different.

Realising that neurodivergent people experienced life harder than most provoked me into wanting to find a way of making life better for those I could support directly or indirectly. I wanted to weave a central panel for the tapestry that told the story of equity and inclusion. That being different was not only welcomed but also embraced and each person was valued for their unique gifts.

Part 2

Chapter 3

Creating neuroinclusive spaces

The stories that you read earlier may resonate with your own experiences of either being neurodivergent or encounters you have had with particular people in your life. I know that I have only become more attuned to difference in the past few years. That inclusion coaching programme was an eye-opener for me. I had never considered intersectionality and how systems and structures can adversely impact someone's life from an early age. For example, growing up in a specific area or going to a particular school may either open or close doors that put you on a life trajectory that you may be powerless to change. My mother understood this and ensured that I went to schools in predominantly white neighbourhoods. In senior school, I was often the only Black child in the class, group, assembly, but the school gave me access to teachers with Oxbridge degrees, a curriculum for intelligent pupils and an expectation that I would go to university.

My school was one of privilege. I do not remember there being any room for or exploration of difference of any kind.

I'm sure that there must have been neurodivergent pupils at my school but I don't know who they were or how they coped with the demanding school environment. Similarly, I went to Imperial College for my first degree, where our lecturers fostered a competitive academic environment. We were told that we were the elite. We were the best. There was no room for divergent thinking there either.

That was 45 years ago. Things are different now and the newly formed Neurodivergence Society at Imperial College is 'dedicated to creating a safe and inclusive environment for neurodivergent individuals' (imperialcollegeunion.org/csp/1376). I want to use what I have learnt through my conversations for this book, interactions with neurodivergent people and my secondary research to do the same.

> **I believe that in any setting that includes neurotypical and neurodivergent people, the onus is on the neurotypical people to make the overtures to create inclusive spaces.**

I believe that in any setting that includes neurotypical and neurodivergent people, the onus is on the neurotypical people to make the overtures to create inclusive spaces. This is because neurodivergent people are already working hard to fit in and conform to societal norms, at great cost to themselves. As a neurotypical person, I recognise that my behaviour can inadvertently impact neurodivergent people negatively. So I need to do the work to understand how that occurs so that I can be instrumental in changing that. I am strongly motivated to do this since I believe my life purpose is 'to create intimate environments so that people thrive'. I recognise that we each have different drivers and topics that we are passionate about, so not everyone will be motivated to create neuroinclusive spaces. And I trust that since you are here, you are someone who wants to be an agent of change in this area.

Generating neuroinclusion is complex because it involves human beings and with that comes unpredictability. We cannot foresee what will happen in any circumstance. What we can do is have some tools and an approach that enable us to navigate a path through with neuroinclusion acting as our North Star. Reflecting on my conversations, experiences and expertise, I have determined a simple framework to draw on to do this.

This scaffold comprises the following elements:

♦ love
♦ safety
♦ social identity
♦ dialogue.

To foster neuroinclusion requires starting from a place of loving others. When I talk about love, I am not referring to romantic love, but the acceptance and cherishing of a person as they are (see Newby & Nunez 2017).

In my conversations, a central theme that emerged was safety. We need to feel safe to have the courage to unveil who we are more fully.

With the foundations of love and safety, we can do the self-exploration to reveal who we are in relation to others, ie unpick our social identities and what that means in terms of how at ease we feel in various groups and social settings.

Bringing a sense of ourselves better enables us to enter into dialogue with one another, which is learning how to think together by seeking to understand. In dialogue we have a basis for joining together to find new ways of being that are inclusive.

Our Three Companions of courage, compassion and wisdom give us the mindset and way of being that permit us to bring this model to life individually and together. Compassion can be seen as a form of love for another. When we love someone it troubles us to see them suffering and we want to lessen or take that pain away. Courage allows us to enter into a space of not knowing, to be vulnerable and willing to reexamine who we are,

> **In dialogue we have a basis for joining together to find new ways of being that are inclusive.**

our beliefs, characteristics and behaviour from a place of self-love and acceptance. When we are open to learning about ourselves and others in dialogue, we can access the collective wisdom that is present and together discover how to be more neuroinclusive.

In the following sections I explore each of these elements in detail.

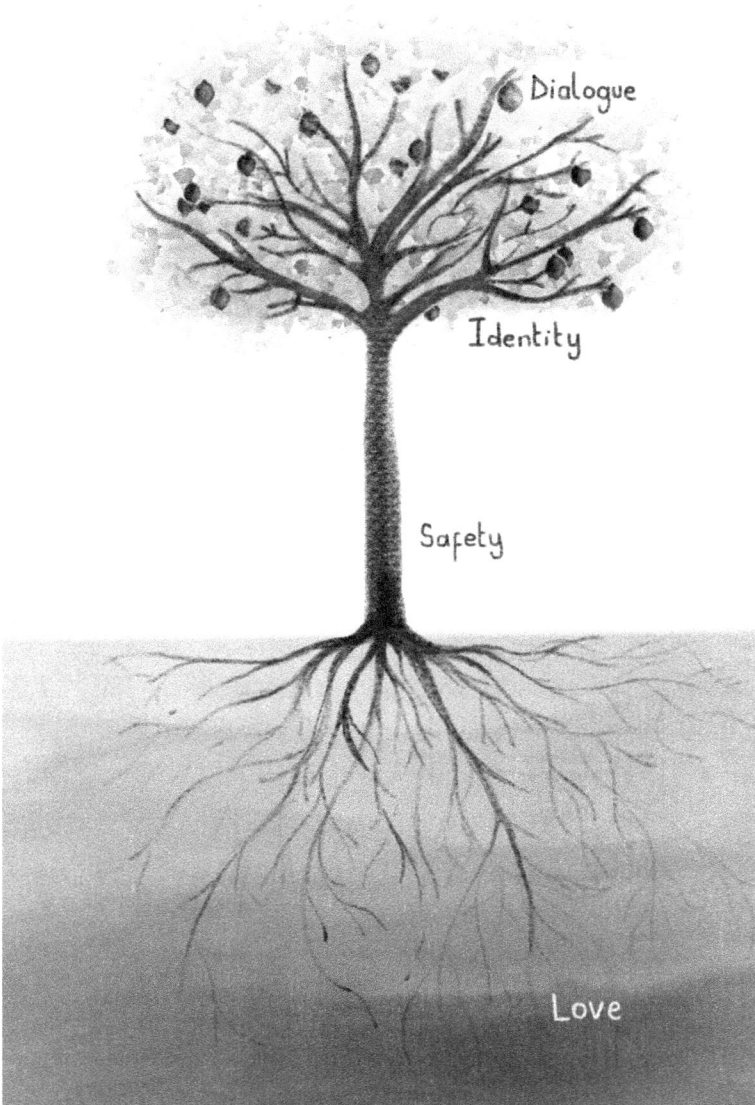

Dialogue

Identity

Safety

Love

Love

The type of love that I believe is essential for crafting neuroinclusion can be described as *agape*. *Agape* comes from Greek and means a profound form of love or charity. It was used in Christianity to describe God's love for humanity and vice versa. It is regarded as the highest form of love because it transcends and persists regardless of circumstance.

In more recent times, the definition of *agape* has been extended, in keeping with the original meaning of charity, to mean unconditional love that is given freely even in difficult circumstances with no expectation of reciprocity (Fleming 2024). *Agape* is filled with kindness and wants only the best for the other person.

- *Agape* accepts others unconditionally, with no expectations of being reciprocated.
- *Agape* sacrifices for the good of the other person. It can sometimes even be viewed as a thankless type of love.
- *Agape* is not envious, proud or boastful.
- *Agape* is patient, giving others grace. It doesn't hold grudges.

You can see that this is different from other forms of love, such as brotherly or romantic love. I inferred that this form of love was present in some of the stories that my interviewees told. The people who showed this were mostly, but not exclusively, mothers. They were unwavering in receiving their children as they are, accepting them unconditionally and putting their child's needs above their own.

Can you imagine how wonderful it must feel like to be

the recipient of *agape?* To know that, regardless of how you feel about yourself, or how you behave towards that person, they will always be there for you? You don't have to mask and pretend to be someone you are not; you can simply be yourself. This is a precious gift that we may not fully appreciate when we have it.

In most of our relationships there is a supposition of reciprocity of the love we are shown. This may be implicit and we are unaware of these hidden expectations until the person becomes angry or disappointed with us because we have not fulfilled them. In a group of friends, or in a family, typically, there is one person who is the glue that keeps everyone together, who makes the overtures for gatherings and ensures everyone in the group stays together. When I have been that person, the one who always reaches out to see how another is doing, I can become fed up that I am the one who does that and can feel resentful towards the others. Then I am not showing *agape*.

The unconditional aspect of *agape* is important because neurodivergent people may not express love in ways that are apparent to others. In several conversations about autistic people, I heard that they showed their love by doing things that were difficult for them to do but that they knew were important for the object of their love – mother, sister, brother, friend, partner. For example, attending the funeral of a close family member, despite feeling much discomfort and not showing any visible signs of grief, to support their parent. Because their parent felt *agape*, their parent recognised the beauty in the act of them being at the funeral rather than feeling disappointed that their child was apparently not grieving.

Practising *agape* not only benefits the recipient but also the giver. It involves being generous, engaging in selfless acts of kindness and developing empathy. Studies have shown that when we do this we increase our levels of oxytocin and endorphins, which are the feel-good hormones, and so we raise our happiness level (Rowland & Curry 2018; Trzeciak et al 2023).

Agape comes from the wellspring of courage, compassion and wisdom, which allow us to think deeply about another and what might be causing their suffering and to present in the best way for them to alleviate that suffering.

An article from the Resilience Lab (2024) provides some tips and practical ways to nurture *agape,* which I have elaborated on in my own words.

♦ **Practise kindness and generosity:** We can look for opportunities to carry out intentional acts of kindness. This can be offering to do shopping for a friend who finds that a chore, giving up some of our free time to spend it with a person who lives alone, sending little messages to lift another's spirits. Over time these everyday acts help to build our empathy and compassion.

♦ **Foster patience and forgiveness:** Embracing *agape* means forgiving others and showing patience, even when it feels difficult. I have heard about amazing acts of forgiveness that are inspiring to me. For example, the special bond formed between Ples Felix and Azim Khamisa after the grandson of Felix killed the son of Khamisa. They showed such courage and strength in the face of tragedy.

Or the South African woman whose son and husband were brutally killed by the same police officer. When asked at the Truth and Reconciliation hearing how justice was to be served, she asked for three things. First, to be taken to the place where her husband had been burnt so she could gather up the dust and give him a decent burial. Second, for the police officer to become her son. She wanted him to spend the day with her twice per month in the ghetto where she lived so she could pour love on him. Finally, she wanted to be escorted across the courtroom to give him a hug so that he would know he was truly forgiven (Foerger 2018). Wow! These are wonderful examples of *agape*.

On a more mundane level, we can show patience when we find someone's behaviour frustrating or irritating. For example, when someone asks what seems like endless questions about what we are requesting them to do, rather than rolling our eyes or snapping at them, we could take a moment to consider that there is a reason why they are probing and take the time to respond.

♦ **Increase our emotional literacy:** Increasing our knowledge of the wide array of emotions that we can experience can support our efforts to understand what we are feeling at key moments and why. For example, we may feel outraged by the way in which someone has treated us. If we take time to reflect on this, we may realise that it's because they have discounted our ideas or we've been overlooked in some way. The underlying emotion is dignity, which is about understanding our value. In this situation, there is a fine balance between being selfless and allowing others to trample over our boundaries. This increased self-awareness will allow us to pause before responding to another and be better able to act out of *agape*.

♦ **Self-compassion:** As we are learning how to show *agape*, we will not get it right in every circumstance. We will get annoyed or angry with someone who we feel is mistreating us. We ignore the plight of a friend in need, telling ourselves that we are too busy. On these occasions, we may feel bad about ourselves. Practising self-compassion will enable us to put these missteps into context and provide the motivation for continuing our efforts to achieve this higher form of love.

♦ **Engage in community service:** Volunteering for causes we believe in allows us to practise selflessness and develop a broader sense of connection with others.

Safety

Maslow's hierarchy of needs is a psychological theory that states that human behaviour is motivated by a desire to fulfil different categories of needs (McLeod 2025). Maslow defined five levels of needs:

1. physiological – breathing, food, water, shelter, clothing, sleep

2. safety and security – health, employment, property, family and social ability
3. love and belonging – friendship, family, intimacy, sense of connection
4. self-esteem – confidence, achievement, respect of others, status
5. self-actualisation – desire to become the most that one can be.

He stated there is a progression from the lowest to highest level of needs, ie we need to fulfil our most basic physiological needs such as hunger, thirst and shelter before we can seek to fulfil the next level of safety and security. That needs to be fulfilled before we move on to love and belonging.

MASLOW'S HIERARCHY
OF NEEDS

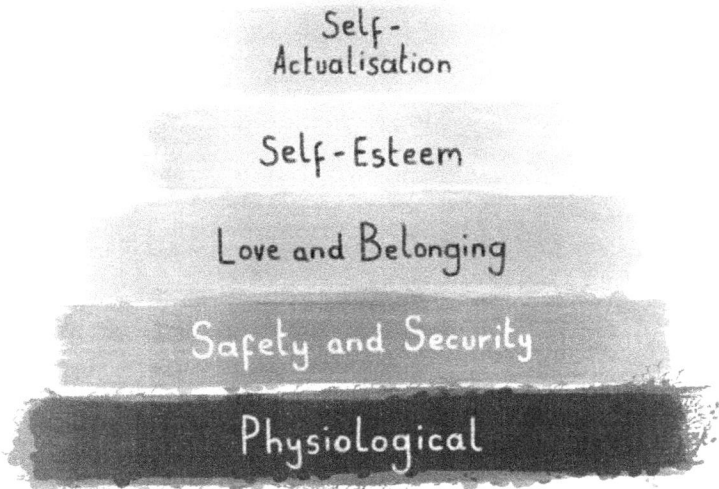

Self-
Actualisation

Self-Esteem

Love and Belonging

Safety and Security

Physiological

Safety needs tend to be met by family and society, so it is not surprising that it has emerged as a theme for neurodivergent people. The parents I spoke with were loving, kind and compassionate. They created a safe home environment where their neurodivergent children could express themselves freely. This was not an easy thing for parents to do and often exhausting. A few of the mothers I spoke with said that there was no downtime for them, particularly if they were neurodivergent themselves. They often expended 'spoons' (a metaphor for the amount of physical or mental energy that a person has available for daily activities and tasks) at work and then came home and consumed more providing the best environment for their neurodivergent children (Neff 2022). I asked one mother how she kept going because she put her family's needs above her own. She replied that it was her faith. Other mothers told me that they were in burnout, and yet I saw that they kept going. They had no option.

I also heard from a few neurodivergent individuals who did not have a safe home environment. They had their physiological needs of food, shelter and water met, but nothing more. They talked about craving signs of love and wanting to belong rather than be othered by their parents. For these individuals, they found safety in neurodivergent communities and friendship groups and in their romantic relationships.

I think creating safety is a fundamental requirement for neuroinclusion. This requirement becomes acute for all disadvantaged persons. It is impossible to be vulnerable and courageous without safety. Having had the experience that I described in the Prologue, I thought carefully about how I could provide a safe environment for people to share their stories with me. I believed it was by allowing my interviewees to feel that they had the power to determine the nature of the conversation.

This began by asking them how comfortable they felt using a video platform, whether they wanted the camera on or off, and agreeing, for those who wanted it, that they could use AI to transcribe the conversation. I also felt it was important that they learnt a little about me so they got a sense of who they were talking to. Before the conversation, I sent them a protocol that described its purpose and what I was asking of them. This allowed them to prepare as much or as little as they wanted to. Regardless, at the start of each conversation,

> **It is impossible to be vulnerable and courageous without safety.**

we spent time talking about what I was looking for, so it was not necessary for them to have read the protocol. My approach was to partner with them to decide how we would conduct the conversation. For example, recognising that some individuals need to express what is on their mind as it arises or they lose that thought, and enquiring whether they were happy with interruptions and questions or wanted to tell their stories in their entirety and for me to hold questions to the end. Interestingly, everyone said they were happy with interruptions. I believe that the other key behaviour was to listen with inquisitiveness rather than having preconceived ideas about what I might hear. I did not know what their tales were about, which meant I needed to listen actively and be present to what was alive in the conversation and our relationship to each other. I was there to listen and learn.

The feedback I received from participants was that my stance was open, curious and invitational, which permitted them to be more relaxed and comfortable sharing their stories. These conversations got me thinking: if I could create a safe environment with strangers, what was it about what I did that enabled that? Would that be replicable in other settings and contexts?

Engendering safety requires us to be compassionate to ourselves and others, and to contemplate what we know about the other person and what they might need. We need to build trust. Trust comes from accepting the other person as they are and meeting the other person where they are. When we connect with love, we are demonstrating that we treasure the other person. This helps them to trust us and develop their affection for themselves. However, this doesn't happen overnight. With repeated expressions of love, the other person will verify the genuineness of our feelings and intentions towards them and reciprocate. In this way we can build a container of safety between us.

Building safety in a relationship also entails us reflecting on what we need so that we can be authentic and form a sincere connection with them. For me, it's spending time getting to know you as a person and the details of your life that go beyond the surface level. When meeting you in a work context for the first time, I like to share the highlights of my career and aspects of my personal history. As our relationship strengthens I reveal more private information to show that I am willing to be vulnerable, open and candid in my relationship with you. I find that when I do that, it establishes a deeper and stronger connection between us that provides the foundation for trust and safety.

Note that for building neuroinclusion, I believe the reverse of Maslow's hierarchy, ie that love comes first. Feeling and showing love for another enables us to then create safety for them and vice versa.

Social identity

How we identify impacts how we show up in various spaces and how safe we feel to be ourselves. For example, I identify more with my intellectual capabilities than my race. Having a PhD from Cambridge gives me instant kudos and credibility with most people. As a result, I feel respected and valued for what I contribute. I am unconcerned that people will dismiss my views. I feel able to speak with authority in many areas and even more comfortable to say I don't know, without feeling that it will adversely affect me.

Contrast this with being a Black African immigrant in the UK, who has a university degree but is a non-native English speaker with a heavy accent. In similar settings to the ones in which I operate, she is dismissed more readily, talked over, ignored, told she has no finesse and she struggles to persuade others to listen to her ideas. From her treatment she has learnt that she is seen as less than those in the dominant group who enjoy many societal advantages. Her natural conclusion is that this is because of her different cultural and ethnic heritage. Understanding that she needs to work harder than many of her peers to gain social standing puts her on her guard and she expends significant energy trying to fit in. She is more likely to remain silent than share her viewpoint.

This experience is often exacerbated for neurodivergent people. For instance, they can acquire a reputation for being rude and uncaring because they challenge others or provide feedback in a direct way. They can be considered as underachieving because they cannot perform tasks in a prescribed way, even though they do well in other aspects of the role or take what is being said literally and do not understand nuance or social cues. Being constantly on the receiving end of these negative messages impacts how safe neurodivergent people feel to be themselves in these contexts.

Reflecting on our identity is not something that we ordinarily do. If you were asked 'Who are you?', what would your answer be? My bet is that your initial response would be to talk about the things that you *do*, for instance *I am a social worker, coach, project director, supply chain professional, marketeer*. It takes deep reflection to consider what makes up our *being*. We can start to explore our answer through looking at the groups to which we feel we do or do not belong – our social identities.

Let's explore this in terms of the nine core identities of:

♦ gender identity – a person's deep-seated felt sense of who they are

- culture/ethnicity – ethnicity relates to our culture, such as sharing a common language, ancestry, national origin, and/or a variety of cultural beliefs
- religion – a person's or a group's beliefs about the existence of God or gods and/or an identification with a particular religion or set of spiritual practices
- race/colour – the concept used to classify humans based on perceived physical characteristics such as skin colour, eye shape and colour, hair texture, body shape and size, and other physical features
- sexual orientation – sexual, emotional, romantic and/or affectional attractions, not necessarily dependent on behaviour
- ability – the diverse array of differences in physical, mental, cognitive, developmental, learning and/or emotional make-up, which also includes mental health and the impact of social experiences such as trauma and surviving abuse
- age – how people are categorised by society's perceptions of different age groups
- education – the level of educational attainment that a person has achieved
- socioeconomic status – commonly conceptualised as one's social standing in society based on income, wealth or poverty. This is often used interchangeably with social class, but social class includes additional factors such as a combination of education, income, occupation, lifestyle and family background.

This can be represented as an identity wheel, such as the one below.

SOCIAL IDENTITY WHEEL

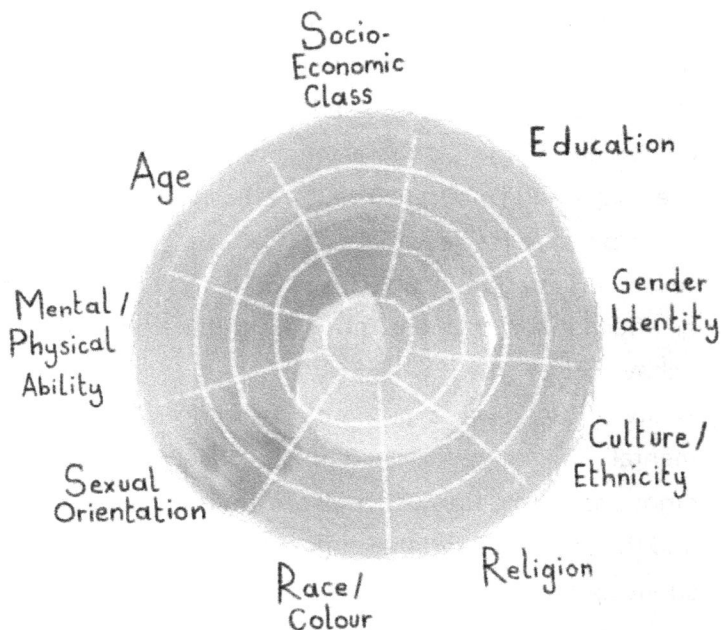

Socio-
Economic
Class

Education

Age

Gender
Identity

Mental /
Physical
Ability

Culture /
Ethnicity

Sexual
Orientation

Religion

Race /
Colour

DEVELOPED BY AMBER MAYES & SUKARI PINNOCK-FITTS (2019)
FOR "THE FIFTH DOMAIN". USED WITH KIND PERMISSION

You can use this wheel to enable you to get a clearer sense of how you relate to various social groups and how these social identities interweave and impact how you feel and behave in different contexts.

For each social identity, contemplate what it means for you. For example, you may express your gender identity as cisgender, transgender, nonbinary, gender fluid and so on. Next, determine whether this social identity forms the majority or minority in the society in which you live. (You could also reflect on whether the group you belong to is dominant or marginalised.) Each concentric circle on the wheel represents 25 per cent and acts as a guide for you to shade in each segment to represent the amount of time you spend thinking about each aspect of your identity. Note: the numbers across wedges are not supposed to add up to 100%. Because of how our identities intersect, we may spend about the same amount of time thinking about two or three identities simultaneously – eg age, gender and race may all be top of mind for a single individual.

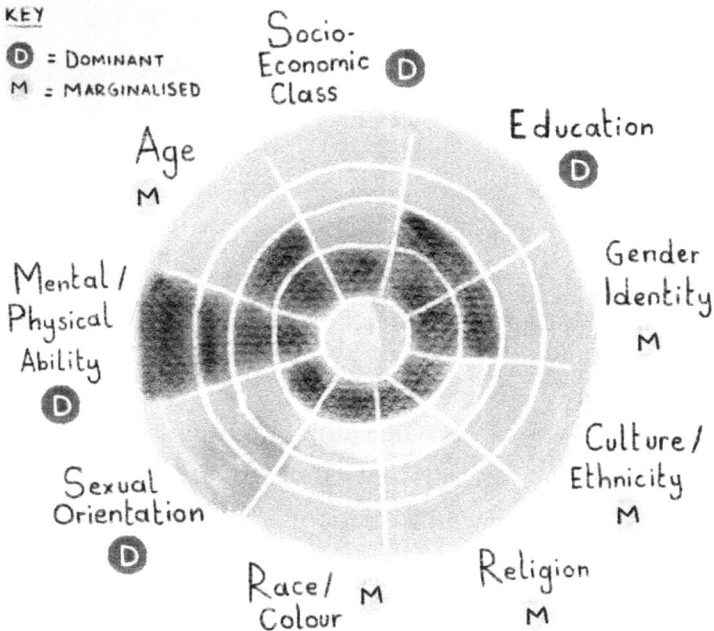

JOAN'S
SOCIAL IDENTITY WHEEL

KEY
D = DOMINANT
M = MARGINALISED

Socio-Economic Class D

Education D

Age M

Gender Identity M

Mental / Physical Ability D

Culture / Ethnicity M

Sexual Orientation D

Religion M

Race / Colour M

Repeat this process for all nine social identities. You will end up with your own version of the identity wheel, which I have constructed for myself above.

It is notable that of the nine social identities, I believe that I fall within the marginalised group for five of them. However, because these are not paramount to me, I feel confident in settings where traditionally my social identity is disadvantaged in some way (for example, being in a male-dominated discipline – chemistry). While I still feel young and vibrant, I am aware that when completing surveys the box I tick for age is almost the highest age category. I'm cognisant that many employers will consider me too old for permanent employment. I think more about how I dress and notice that my hemlines are getting longer. I'm fortunate that I'm in a sweet spot of being seen with expertise and wisdom while looking years younger, so I'm not automatically written off because of my age. In fact, I am fearless when going into new settings and engaging in difficult conversations. So, while age hasn't been a significant aspect of my identity hitherto, in the past five years I have become more aware of its significance to me.

When we ponder how we are in each of these categories, we weave together a story of who we are.

'I am a spiritual, white, middle-aged, well-educated man. I grew up in a multicultural neighbourhood and had friends from different ethnic backgrounds. This has shaped my world view and how I engage with my work colleagues. I am more patient than some of my peers who had more affluent upbringings. I am generally fit and well and try to still play team sports.'

'I am a Nigerian, professional woman who needs to be a role model for other young women who aspire to be leaders. Family and culture are very important to me and some of the European norms seem strange to me. For example, I would never be disrespectful to my parents. It is expected that I will study and work hard to attain a good profession. I'm very proud of my culture and want to display it prominently in the way I dress, do my hair, etc.'

'I am disabled because I am neurodivergent. I have to constantly advocate for myself and my needs because others are unwilling to put the effort in to learn about neurodivergence. I struggle with social cues and am literal in my thinking and what I say. This can lead to others taking offence. I'm tired of having to educate others on the ways that neurodivergence can manifest itself. I'm young but feel that my life is slipping away because I'm not given the chances to try out different things by my peers.'

Review your identity wheel. What is the story that you are telling yourself?

When we meet people, we make assumptions about who they are based on our stereotypes and biases. We organise them and ourselves into groups to help us make sense of our world. We tend to emphasise the similarities between people of the same group and amplify the differences between groups. Because we rarely spend time in organisations getting to know each other as individuals, we form a view of who people are from external appearances – how they speak, dress, carry themselves, where they live, their name, etc. However, we may have a faulty perception of others. And this picture affects how we feel and behave towards others and vice versa.

Take for example, team meetings. Typically, there are one or two people who take up most of the airtime. Each of us will make up a story about these individuals based on our experiences in other settings and behave accordingly. If I don't know the individual well, I may regard them as opinionated, wanting to score points, intimidating. In this case, I'll be wary about publicly challenging them and may hold views about their seemingly aggressive nature. Conversely, if I take time to get to know the individual, I may discover that I'm wrong in my assumption. They may struggle with public speaking, hate being in the spotlight or feel it is their duty to challenge ideas that don't make sense or seem to contain flaws.

> **So a key role for leaders in organisations is to invest time building relationships with their team members and fostering psychological safety in their team.**

Creating reflective spaces in which individuals can explore who they are and learn about their colleagues is not easy. It requires a level of vulnerability that most people are unwilling to embrace unless they feel safe. So a key role for leaders in organisations is to invest time building relationships with their team members and fostering psychological safety in their team.

When we appreciate how our social identities influence how we behave in different settings, we can be mindful about how we show up. I encourage you, dear reader, to develop contemplative practices that support you in uncovering the multitude of social identities that you embody. Explore questions such as, 'When do you feel most at ease? Who are you with? What do you know about them? How well do you relate to them? What is it about them that allows you to feel at ease? What does this allow you to do?'

And contrast these answers with your reflections on the situations where you feel unease.

What are you learning about your in- and out-groups?

Our out-groups are the spaces where we need to put in more effort to create neuroinclusion. This is because we will tend to judge and treat people who are in our out-groups more negatively than people in our in-groups. As the various journeys that I have described earlier show, neurodivergent people are often judged and placed in the out-groups of their neurotypical colleagues, not intentionally but by the nature of unconscious biases, expectations and the arbitrariness of the social contract and the unwritten rules regarding behaviour. Having deeper awareness of who we are permits us to ponder who we are in relation to others. This is a step towards determining whether we want to change how we are with people in our out-groups.

Having insight into our identities and our biases is one step towards creating neuroinclusion. However, we may not have all the pieces to complete that jigsaw puzzle. Consider how many individuals are late-diagnosed as being neurodivergent.

How can they fully understand who they are if they are not aware of an important facet of their being? Many of my interviewees talked about feeling that there was something wrong with them or that they were stupid and that when they were diagnosed they could understand themselves better.

Reflection alone is not enough to gain this insight because we can get stuck in our thoughts. Having the support of at least one other person with whom we can reflect permits us to examine our ideas and beliefs regarding what we believe to be true about ourselves and others. Their role can be to gently challenge us by asking questions that cause us to ponder on how our social identities and values have formed, how our experiences have changed our outlook, whether the relative weighting we give to each social identity is still serving us.

> **Having the support of at least one other person with whom we can reflect permits us to examine our ideas and beliefs regarding what we believe to be true about ourselves and others.**

Dialogue

I am convinced that dialogue is at the heart of generating neuroinclusion. When I refer to dialogue I mean an exchange where the participants seek to understand each other rather than score points. Dialogue comes from Greek roots, *dia* = through, *logos* = word, and has come to mean a conversation between two or more people. I think we can be in dialogue with ourselves, one other person or many others. Dialogue is a word that is overused today. Often when people talk about dialogue they are referring to discussions where individuals come together to speak about what is on their mind. The intent is to bring to the surface things that are not being said, which may be pertinent to solving an issue. This is laudable and I encourage people to do that. What I notice, however, is that individuals tend to take up positions and advocate for their point of view. Often the opportunity to learn together, which is an essential aspect of dialogue, is lost.

My interviewees gave examples of conversations they had that helped them to better understand and make sense of what was happening. For some late-diagnosed neurodivergent people, there was someone whom they trusted – a loving partner, coach, mother, compassionate teacher – who gently suggested that they might be neurodivergent. This person wanted to support and help the neurodivergent person to thrive in the world. Having someone

When I refer to dialogue I mean an exchange where the participants seek to understand each other rather than score points.

who is in their corner is crucial for neurodivergent people not only to survive but flourish.

The mothers I spoke to intuitively provided a loving environment in which to explore meltdowns, antisocial behaviour, feelings of sadness and depression. They spoke to their neurodivergent children about how the world worked, their impact on others and how some behaviour was not OK (for example, hitting).

William Isaacs describes dialogue as a 'shared inquiry, a way of thinking and reflecting together.' He states that collective action emerges from shared meaning, which flows from the genuine common understanding that arises in dialogue. Dialogue helps to 'uncover the undiscussed thinking of people.' I agree with him that you need to cultivate dialogue within yourself and then role model it for others before applying that approach to others. When done properly, dialogue offers a setting that permits differences to be surfaced and reflected upon in a safe way that allows participants to start to make sense of these differences. Isaacs states that 'the intention of dialogue is to reach new understanding and, in doing so, to form a totally new basis from which to think and act.' This can lead to new possibilities that might not have occurred without dialogue. Dialogue is a place where healing can begin/occur. Dialogue impacts how people act together! (Isaacs 1999)

> **Dialogue is a place where healing can begin/occur.**

Why I deem dialogue to be central to creating neuroinclusion is because its purpose is to evoke insight: dialogue helps participants to see something they already know in a different and new light. We each come to the figurative table with our own perceptions of how we need to behave and interact with each other. Dialogue is an opportunity to reexamine this. For example, how often when we greet someone are we interested in how they are? That question is a habit with no substance. Neurotypical people understand that in most situations the required answer is 'Fine, thank you. How are you?' On the rare occasion that someone truly wants to know, they will not accept this rote answer and will enquire again. However, if you are autistic it takes some missteps to realise that you are not required to answer literally with an account of how you are really doing. In meetings, groups establish their own norms: for example, it's acceptable to be late for meetings because we have overrun during a previous one. This is disrespectful to the people who are punctual and unfathomable for some neurodivergent colleagues, who like to know the exact time of the meeting, the purpose, duration, etc. Not understanding this unwritten rule can be baffling for neurodivergent people and result in them being seen as being difficult to work with despite delivering their own work to a high standard.

> **Dialogue helps participants to see something they already know in a different and new light.**

There are many assumptions that we make without questioning why. Dialogue affords us the opportunity to reflect on exclusive practices that may only suit some individuals.

While dialogue seems like a simple solution to create neuroinclusive spaces, it is hard and takes a lot of work to succeed. This is not something that can happen overnight and it can take months or years to practice this effectively. Each person has to want to do the inner work it takes to be in dialogue with themselves and others.

Cultivating dialogue

Isaacs has identified four behaviours that support the promotion of dialogue:

♦ listening
♦ respecting
♦ suspending
♦ voicing.

I explore each of these in the following sections.

Listening

Much has been written about listening, and there are numerous models of what constitutes effective listening. I approach this from my perspective as a coach and facilitator of learning. When we truly listen to another, magic happens. The person listened to feels that they have been given the gift of your full attention. How often are we enthralled by another human being? Mostly, we afford them some of our consciousness but our mind may be somewhere else.

At the basic level, we listen to the content of what someone is *saying*. What words are they using? When we are attending more to them, we listen to different channels. The second channel relates to the *music*. How is the person speaking, ie the tone, speed, emphasis? Listening to the music can give us clues about what is significant for the speaker. If a speaker is talking at one speed and slows down during the conversation, it may mean that they are thinking about something, they are processing what they are saying as they are speaking or they may be questioning what they are saying.

A third channel is to listen for the *dance*. We listen with our eyes as well as our ears. What are the non-verbal signals that the speaker is giving? Are they saying one thing while their face is conveying something else? What can we make of hand gestures that accompany the words?

You can see that there is a lot more information that we can glean by paying attention to what the speaker is communicating. However, we need to be careful in our interpretation of non-verbal cues and what they mean. For example, most neurotypical people believe that you demonstrate that you are listening and paying attention to another person by making eye contact. However, many autistic people find it uncomfortable to make eye contact. They try to do this because that is the convention and what is expected of them. Doing so makes it hard to process information and

> **We need to be careful in our interpretation of non-verbal cues and what they mean.**

their thoughts simultaneously, which further exacerbates their difficulties in engaging socially. Another challenge with trying to read the body language of a neurodivergent person is that they are constantly masking, so unless they become dysregulated, it will be impossible to know that they are feeling distressed. Going back to the Prologue, I had no idea that the autistic participant who went back to his hotel room and cried was feeling distraught. Being curious about the speaker as we listen to them will help us to dispel our customary interpretations of what they are communicating.

When we are listening it's important to listen for what is

being said and what is not being said. If we spot inconsistencies in what the person is saying we can enquire about these from a place of inquisitiveness. In dialogue we need to listen at a deeper level to the underlying dilemma that a person may be exploring. We may wonder about what someone is not saying. For example, they may say something is important to them, a core value, and that doesn't feature in what they later say. Gently pointing this out might help the speaker to reexamine their beliefs and assumptions.

As the listener, asking a simple, open question (questions that begin with 'Who? What? Where? When? How?') and listening without interrupting allows the other person to process their thoughts and unlock new insights and ideas. But how often do we do that? Often we listen just long enough to give our counterargument or to prove our point. We are not really listening.

> **Being curious about the speaker as we listen to them will help us to dispel our customary interpretations of what they are communicating.**

In conversations, we make assumptions all the time and act as though those assumptions are true without ever verifying them. This can lead us to create a story in our head about what is happening in a conversation that is a fabrication on our part. We also infer something based on what we do know. For example, she spoke loudly to me. I infer from that behaviour that she's criticising me or angry with me. As a result, I become defensive and either withdraw and become sulky or I further justify what I said.

The visual below illustrates what happens in the ladder of inference, which shows how we act on the fantasies that we invent.

THE LADDER OF INFERENCE

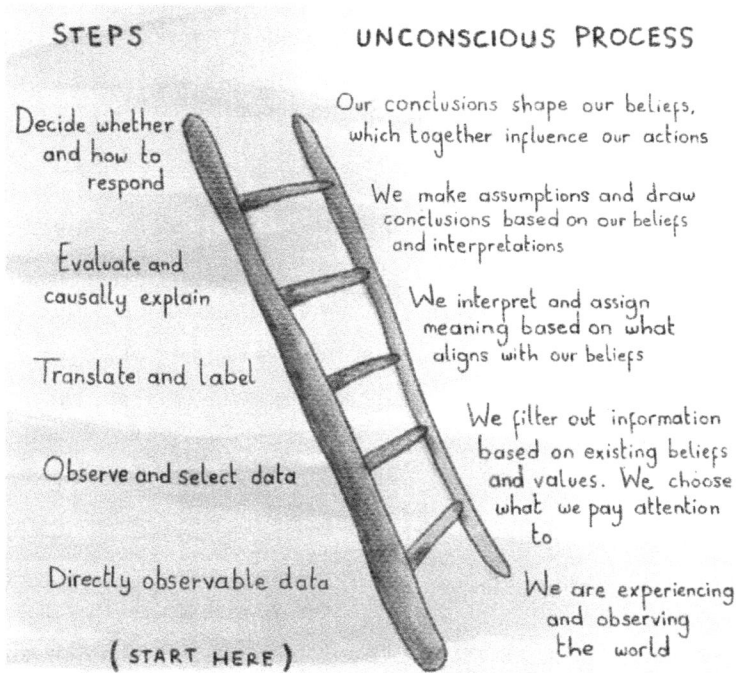

STEPS

Decide whether and how to respond

Evaluate and causally explain

Translate and label

Observe and select data

Directly observable data

(START HERE)

UNCONSCIOUS PROCESS

Our conclusions shape our beliefs, which together influence our actions

We make assumptions and draw conclusions based on our beliefs and interpretations

We interpret and assign meaning based on what aligns with our beliefs

We filter out information based on existing beliefs and values. We choose what we pay attention to

We are experiencing and observing the world

Let me bring this to life with an example.

Starting at the bottom of the ladder, I'm in a meeting and can see where people are sitting, what they are doing, whether they are speaking, keeping quiet, etc *(directly observable data)*.

Moving to the next step in the ladder, I look around the room as I propose an idea that I want the rest of the group to implement. As I am speaking, I notice someone frown. I believe that this individual is resistant to my ideas *(observe and select data)*. I interpret their frown as silent disagreement with what I am suggesting *(translate and label)*.

Moving up the ladder, I assume that this individual thinks that my idea is flawed and will not get on board. They will be vociferous in their objections, which will negatively influence others in the meeting *(evaluate and causally explain)*.

I lack confidence and feel unsure of my standing in this group, so become more tentative in my request to them. Rather than asking for a volunteer to pilot the concept, I say that I hope someone will be willing to give this idea a try *(decide whether and how to respond)*.

I will probably leave the meeting with my belief reinforced that the individual is always going against my ideas.

From this example, you will see that at no point have I asked the individual who frowned what they thought of my proposal. I'm guessing that the frown was in response to what I said but it could be completely unrelated. They may have felt a moment of discomfort which caused their facial expression or suddenly remembered something that they needed to do. If we don't enquire, we will not dispel myths that we are holding or uncover new information that could prove valuable.

I am world class at making inferences and acting on them.

This is not conducive to promoting dialogue in either group settings or one-on-one conversations, because we end up misinterpreting what someone has said or meant. How often have you thought that someone was fierce, stern or difficult, only to discover later that they were warm and kind and that you were the intimidating one? Or they were surprised that they came across in the way that you perceived?

Deep listening is a skill that takes practice. It is noticeable when I run exercises to develop listening skills that participants report that they find it hard to sit in silence for three minutes. Our natural tendency is to comment on what we are hearing and ask follow-up questions. While this can be useful, at times it is more powerful for us to hold the space for someone else and not insert ourselves into their process. Simply being present for the other person is often enough for profound learning to occur.

We need to be genuine in our desire to give space to the speaker to reflect on and process thoughts and feelings that are emerging for them in the conversation. By holding silence we allow them to access deeper, below-the-surface sensations that give rise to new insights for them and us.

To do this, we need to be genuine in our desire to give space to the speaker to reflect on and process thoughts and feelings that are emerging for them in the conversation. By holding silence we allow them to access deeper, below-the-surface sensations that give rise to new insights for them and us.

Respecting

Isaacs describes respecting as a sense of honouring or deferring to someone – to see the person in their entirety rather than aspects of them. Sawubona is a beautiful Zulu greeting that translates as 'I see you'. It also carries the deeper meaning of recognising each person's worth and dignity – 'by seeing you, I bring you into being', by seeing all of them – their hopes, fears, strengths, weaknesses, joys, pains.

Related to this is *ubuntu,* which is a philosophy that emphasises our humanity and interconnectedness in society.

> **Sawubona is a beautiful Zulu greeting that translates as 'I see you'. It also carries the deeper meaning of recognising each person's worth and dignity.**

It is not easily translated into English. However, one phrase that captures the essence of this belief system is 'I am because you are'. *Ubuntu* encompasses the interdependence of human beings on each other and conveys a sense of responsibility to each other and the world around us. Feeling this way towards our fellow human beings is fundamental to respecting them.

We can cultivate respect for others by regarding everyone we meet as being a teacher from whom we can learn. This is not easy to do when we have different values, a different outlook or disagree with someone. Respecting others requires us to be curious about and to listen for what is being said and not said. We can adopt some questions during the conversation to help us do this. Such as, 'What is happening right now? Am I seeing the bigger picture? How does what I am seeing and hearing fit into the wider context?'

Another aspect of respecting is to honour others' boundaries. This means we accept that each person has different needs and when they say 'no' to us that they mean it. When we respect others' boundaries in dialogue, we do not push them more than they are willing to go. For example, we may notice that they are avoiding giving a direct response to a request for information. Respecting them means that we are sensitive to that reticence and do not insist that they answer the question. There's a fine balance to be had in this situation because noticing the reticence may bring to the surface underlying issues that will enhance the dialogue and greater understanding. We can learn what is appropriate in each situation by observing the interactions between people and testing our inferences by asking the individual if this is something that they would like to explore. A risky move, I admit. However, if

> **We can cultivate respect for others by regarding everyone we meet as being a teacher from whom we can learn. This is not easy to do when we have different values, a different outlook or disagree with someone.**

we have created a safe container, while it would take courage to ask, we can apply our wisdom about timing, whether to do it in public or private and consider how to do this with compassion. Offering the question lightly as an invitation gives the speaker permission to decline without feeling bad about it.

I think it's also worth pointing out that there's a fine line between not intruding on someone and distancing yourself. For example, when someone is bereaved, do you become silent because you know that they are dealing with a lot of things and feeling the need to respond to you would be one more thing on their pile (respecting a boundary), or do you become silent because you don't know what to say to them (distancing)? The simplest way to be sure that we are honouring someone's boundaries is to ask them.

> **Another aspect of respecting is to honour others' boundaries. This means we accept that each person has different needs and when they say 'no' to us that they mean it. When we respect others' boundaries in dialogue, we do not push them more than they are willing to go.**

To respect others, we first need to learn how to respect ourselves. Self-respect can be defined as seeing our worth in the world, honouring our needs and desires and maintaining our dignity. We appreciate who we are, live by our values and establish clear boundaries for how we want to be treated. Our self-respect develops through lived experiences and it can be hard to change acquired beliefs and habits. We benefit from acknowledging our past without being chained to it so that we can foster meaningful change.

Here are a few ideas to reset or develop our self-respect (Davis 2024):

1. **Reflect on your values** – Spend time pondering what is important to you. What are the standards of behaviour that you want to uphold? How are you living in accordance

with your values? If there is a mismatch between what you ascribe to and what you do, what is the reason for this? What actions can you take so that you live more in tune with your values?

2. **Examine your relationships** – Who are the people that you spend your time with outside of work? How well treated do you feel in these relationships? Do your friends and family treat you with kindness, support and affirm you, particularly when times are hard? Are they critical of you and your needs? How do you feel when you are with them? If you find that the people you choose to spend your leisure time with are pulling you down, what can you do to redress the situation? How can you assert some boundaries regarding how you want them to treat you? If they seem unwilling to change, are you prepared to walk away? Find people whose company you enjoy, who you feel good to be around, who get you.

> To respect others, we first need to learn how to respect ourselves. Self-respect can be defined as seeing our worth in the world, honouring our needs and desires and maintaining our dignity. We appreciate who we are, live by our values and establish clear boundaries for how we want to be treated.

3. **Practise self-care** – When we think about self-care we think about physical things, such as resting, exercising, eating healthily. There are other forms of self-care, including professional, which relates to our experience at

work; emotional, noticing our feelings without judgement; psychological, taking care of our minds; and spiritual (connecting with or to something bigger than ourselves, such as purpose, the environment).

4. **Practise self-compassion** – Kristen Neff identified three elements of self-compassion: mindfulness (noticing our emotions with interest and acceptance), common humanity (acknowledging that we are not alone in our distress and it's human to err), self-kindness (treating ourselves the way we would behave towards a loved one in a similar situation). These elements are expressed variously in what she describes as tender and fierce self-compassion. Tender self-compassion is accepting ourselves with loving kindness while fierce self-compassion is the force we need to act, such as asking for what we need, protecting ourselves, asserting boundaries, establishing healthy habits.

5. **Challenge negative thoughts** (Gupta 2022) – Most of us have an inner critic who mentally beats us up when something has not gone the way that we would like. Being critical and unkind to ourselves is not motivating; it simply serves to make us feel bad about ourselves. It's hard to respect ourselves when our inner voice is berating us. For some neurodivergent people, developing self-respect can be hard. They tend to distrust their intuition because they've had a lifetime of negative messages that essentially tell them that they are made wrong. They become people pleasers and allow others to violate their boundaries because they want to be loved and accepted. Having

supporters who enable neurodivergent people to discover their dignity is a vital part of creating equity and inclusion.

Suspending

The third quality for dialogue is called suspending (Isaacs 1999). It is about first noticing our thoughts and reactions to what is happening in the dialogue without either sticking rigidly to them or denying them, and then becoming aware of the processes that led to these thoughts and reactions. It's similar to the mindfulness component of self-compassion.

Suspending is about deeply enquiring into what is driving our thoughts. To do this we need to stay wise and curious about what is happening in the present moment. When we are usually in conversation, we want to fix, correct or problem-solve what we believe is the issue. Think of the clichéd story of a woman describing a situation to her partner and he immediately tells her what to do. Often our job as leaders and managers is to solve problems at work. So when we switch into a role that is supporting reflection and learning, it can be hard to feel that we are doing something of value since there is not an immediate tangible outcome from our efforts.

To practise suspending, we must let go of knowing and being certain. If we release our hold on being right, we can gain access to other viewpoints and wonder about them. Isaacs suggests some questions to help us be less certain: Why are you so sure about this? What is leading you to hold on to it so intensely? What could be the payoff to you? What would happen if you let it go? What is at risk/might you lose if you do? What do you fear you would lose?

Additionally, we can move away from binary, 'either/ or' thinking and try to integrate polarised viewpoints and embrace the 'grey'. What do I mean here? It is natural to believe something is either right or wrong, black or white. For example, there is a prevailing view that people need to have their video cameras on during online meetings and need to face the camera. If that is not the case, we tend to assume that they are not paying attention and doing other things while being on the call. That is black-and-white thinking. The grey space is understanding that people may have valid reasons for not switching on their cameras but are still engaged. For example, they may not want to expose their home environment to their colleagues. Given that this book is about neuroinclusion, it would be remiss of me not to mention the difficulty some neurodivergent people have with video calls. A few of my conversations were conducted with cameras off. The benefit of doing this was that there were fewer distractions for us both and we could concentrate on the conversation and what was being communicated.

Reframing how we see things is another way of suspending our judgement. For example, I remember encountering a health and safety officer in the factory where I worked. He tended to focus on what we were doing wrong, which came across as being critical and unhelpful. I decided to see him in a different light, ie that there was a lot of good in him, he had a lot of expertise and he was trying to protect us. Once I recast my picture of him, I was able to approach him in a collaborative way and ask for his help, which he was only too happy to give. In meetings of any kind, at work and in our personal lives, we form opinions of others based on our impressions of them, on how they present themselves, how they speak, what they say, how they behave and so forth. Remember the ladder of inference? Suspending also means that we hold our judgement of others and remain open minded to who they are and what might be underlying drivers for their behaviour. Asking ourselves questions such as 'What am I missing? How have things come to be this way? What is the question beneath the question?' can be helpful here.

In addition to suspension at the individual level, Isaacs talks about suspension in groups as the ability to surface issues that impact all in the group in a way that they can reflect on them. It's about interrupting habitual patterns so that the group can see new possibilities, such as a different way of working. It's about approaching the group with curiosity and observing what is happening in the group as a whole. It's important not to personalise emotions but to see what is happening with others. It's about observing not only what is changing but what is staying the same.

Voicing

The fourth behaviour for dialogue is what Isaacs calls voicing. He believes voicing is 'one of the most challenging aspects of genuine dialogue'. It takes courage to reveal what is true for you regardless of what might be true for others. To do this, it is important to enquire within, 'What needs to be expressed now?', and listen to yourself. Tune into your inner voice and intuition rather than what you have internalised as the 'right' way to behave.

It's about allowing what is forming internally to take shape before articulating it. We can achieve this by learning to be still and not rushing to fill the silence. When a coach holds silence for their client, the latter can access deeper thoughts and feelings and articulate these. We can learn to do this for ourselves. When we slow down sufficiently we can trust that our inner wisdom will provide us with the right words to say at the right moment, if we allow it.

> **On countless occasions I have witnessed people's surprise at what they articulate when they are given the space to do so. And the vocalisation was something that they were unaware was bubbling under the surface.**

I have been hosting online conversations for individuals with a common interest in the Three Companions since the first Covid-19 lockdown in March 2020. A couple of the ground rules that I established at the start seem pertinent here. One was that each person could come as they are; they didn't have to pretend in any way. If they were feeling some discomfort, it was OK to express it in the group. The other one was that each person would take a turn speaking on the topic we selected for that week and could say whatever felt relevant to them. Over the years we have covered topics such as generosity, happiness, languishing, grief, hope, asserting our needs while retaining important relationships, teasing others. There is no prescribed order for speaking and, in each session, one or two individuals elect to take a later turn to allow themselves time to consider what they want to say. These conversations are conducted at a pace that permits reflection and for each person to have a voice. On countless occasions I have witnessed people's surprise at what they articulate when they are given the space to do so. And the vocalisation was something that they were unaware was bubbling under the surface.

Finding your voice can feel scary. It can take bravery and the willingness to be vulnerable. One way to do this is to ask yourself, 'Who will play my music if I don't play it myself?' I find this to be a wise question. How many times have you walked away from a conversation wishing you had had the pluck to speak up? What stopped you? It's about finding the nerve to offer it. We should consider, 'What's at stake if we don't express ourselves?'

We tend to think through and plan what we are going to say, so improvising feels risky. A good analogy for me is jazz. Often the musicians don't know what they are going to play beyond a basic melody. They feel the mood and the music and play the notes that flow through their body. The musicians play the right music for that moment. It is unique and there will not be another instance like it. When the musicians come together to play that tune the next time, it will be different because they will feel different, the mood will be different and what needs to be expressed will be different. And the music will be just as sweet as the time before.

This is the same for dialogue. Each moment is unique. There will never be the same opportunity to express what we are feeling in any particular moment. Next time the group meets, the conditions will be different because each person will be different. They won't be feeling the same way, may be on different form, have other thoughts and ideas, be facing different issues. These all affect how each person shows up. So, each time the group meets, it's a new group on some level. *Carpe diem,* seize the day, is a good motto to adopt when in dialogue.

Chapter 4

Bringing it all together

So, how do we bring the various aspects of the framework outlined in Chapter 3 together to generate more neuro-inclusive spaces at work?

I want to illustrate how we can generate neuroinclusion using these four building blocks of love, safety, social identity and dialogue through a series of gatherings in which my original cast of characters are joined by some new players. They are convening for a series of sessions to explore the topic of neuroinclusion in the hope that through their dialogue they will generate new thinking together.

My intent is that the following scenes show some of the steps that you could take to create neuroinclusive events, such as workshops, committee meetings, task force sessions, society forums, working parties. Note that this is an example and not the only way to build neuroinclusion.

Introducing the new characters

♦ Olivia, 60, is a coach and diversity, equity and inclusion expert. She has her own business, primarily facilitating individual and group learning. She works with big corporates supporting their leaders and teams to be more effective and inclusive, coaches senior leaders and executives and runs workshops and webinars on diversity and inclusion. Olivia also does some pro bono work in coaching and facilitation for people and sectors who would not ordinarily be able to access her services. She has a passion for inclusion and belonging and facilitating dialogue. Olivia is the convenor and facilitator of this dialogue group.

♦ Bhavya, 39, is a successful architect. She worked for a small practice for eight years and felt she had plateaued there. Three years ago, she decided to establish her own practice. She had a good network and had built a reputation for interesting designs and high-quality work. Bhavya now employs three junior staff. She has self-diagnosed as being autistic and has developed strategies to cope with life. On occasion she feels that her interactions with her staff and clients are a bit off and she wants to better understand how she can engage in ways that are less intimidating and more empowering for others.

♦ Bryn, 32, is originally from Wales. He moved to Bristol when he went to university and later settled there. He is a research assistant at the university. He has an older brother who is autistic. Bryn always looked out for him at school but chose to get away from home as soon as he could to feel free to live his own life. He goes home occasionally and spends time with his brother then. Otherwise, they have limited contact. Having got out from under the shadow of his brother and his parents, Bryn is ready to explore neurodiversity on his own terms. The dialogue group is intriguing to him because it is different from what he has encountered before.

♦ Finn, 45, tests and writes reviews for a range of electronic items such as headphones for specialist magazines. He regards this as his dream job as it fits with his special interests. He has been doing the job for 13 years and still enjoys it. He works from home and is sent the products to review. This is ideal because he doesn't enjoy busy office environments and can indulge in doing deep research about each product. He has to be careful not to go into too much detail in his reviews. This skill has taken him years to hone as he was usually so excited to share his knowledge. With strong direction and feedback from his managers, he has learnt to curb his enthusiasm in his writing while being ready to discuss the intricacies and merits of each design with anyone who will listen. He knows that he is lucky and that some of his neurodivergent friends have more challenging work experiences. Finn was late-diagnosed as neurodivergent and wants to learn from others' experiences and contribute to making the world a fairer place.

♦ Naomi, 53, is an executive assistant to the CEO of a mid-sized organisation. She believes that her boss is neurodivergent. Although they have never discussed it, Naomi has witnessed times when her boss has become emotionally dysregulated and spiralled into catastrophising about what has happened (for example, a difficult conversation with a member of her exec team). Naomi has had to calm her boss down on several occasions. On occasion she has become a motherly figure, providing a shoulder to cry on. Naomi has also seen her boss's brilliance – her ability to lead the organisation through turbulent times with a clarity and decisiveness that is rarely seen. She suspects there are others in the organisation who are neurodivergent. Naomi wants to understand more about neurodivergence to support her boss and them more effectively. She has attended some webinars but is hungry to do something that would effect change.

◆ Rowan, 28, is dyslexic. He got through school using bravado. His creativity and engaging character garnered praise from teachers and friends who helped him with some of his schoolwork. He enjoyed reading, although he struggled with heavy texts. He learnt that he could take information in more easily by listening to podcasts or recorded classes and watching videos. He works as a graphic designer for a packaging company. Rowan has not had the courage to speak up about some of the difficulties he faces, such as getting lost in conversations because his thoughts have gone on a tangent from the main point and he has forgotten what they were talking about. His interest in neuroinclusion is to help him be more courageous in asking for help.

◆ Sofia, 23, has recently joined the ranks of the employed. She works as a business analyst for a bank. She enjoys and is good at her work but finds the office environment too noisy and distracting. Her preference would be to work from home but she is required to go into the office full time. She often books a quiet room at the office so she can do her work without many interruptions. She likes her line manager and gets on well with her colleagues. Beyond that she keeps to herself and says little in public meetings. Sofia would like to have more friends and tries to join in the work social activities but often leaves early because she finds them so uncomfortable. Sofia has been persuaded by Olivia to join this group so she can build her confidence to speak out in groups in a safe environment.

A reminder of the original cast members

♦ Limbani, 51, is the mother of Xavier. She switched from going out to full-time work to working part time from home so that she could give Xavier the care and nurturing that he needed. She had struggled to be heard when she initially raised concerns about his developmental needs and had to fight hard to get the assistance that he required at school. With the help of a team of special education needs professionals, Limbani received the support that she and Xavier needed. As a result she has grown in confidence in trusting her instincts as a mother. Having fought for Xavier for much of his young life, Limbani is keen to be part of a community that wants to effect change that improves the understanding and acceptance of neurodivergence among the population at large, and educators in particular, so that other parents don't have to go through the battles that she did.

◆ Nathan, 51, is Limbani's husband and the father of Xavier. He had the common fatherly expectations that his son would be popular and good at sports. He had adapted to Xavier's needs but missed the social interactions that he'd had with his family. In going through the diagnostic process for Xavier, Nathan uncovered his own neurodivergence. Over time he better understood himself and Xavier and was able to feel pride in his son. Nathan wants to share his story and has started writing about his experiences so that others can gain insight into why he behaves as he does. He has agreed to join this group because this has potential for grassroots action in the community.

◆ Xavier, 20, is the son of Limbani and Nathan. He was diagnosed as autistic with ADHD when he was ten. Prior to this, he had found the noisy classroom environment challenging. He had become overwhelmed and had frequent meltdowns at home where he felt safe after masking for so long during the school day. His life changed once he and his needs were understood and he got the support that he required. He developed coping strategies to help him navigate the world. He is in his final year at university. Xavier likes the idea that there is someone (Olivia) who wants to facilitate change. He has not found life easy but has been sustained by his parents, teachers and learning support assistants. He's one of the lucky ones. However, he is aware of some young people on the periphery of his circle who are less fortunate. They do not have a nurturing home environment and face more struggles as a result. Xavier would like to support them better but is unsure how to do that. He hopes that this group will help him to think about that.

- Phoebe, 48, is the partner of Myles. She met Myles at work. They started out as colleagues and friends. Their relationship evolved to a romantic involvement and they moved in together five years previously. Phoebe discovered the joys and challenges of living with Myles due to his spiky profile. It took a while for her to believe that he was autistic and dispel the beliefs she had previously held about autism. Phoebe wants to learn how to balance getting her needs met while supporting Myles.

- Myles, 46, is the partner of Phoebe. He is autistic. He is worldly wise and enjoys engaging in long conversations about a wide range of topics. His passion is music, which he has studied for most of his life. He seems to be the life and soul of the party, but this is a learned script that he enacts, which costs him a lot of energy. He loves Phoebe but sometimes has a disproportionately angry response to something that she does and then feels contrite afterwards. Myles is less convinced that there is a problem. He is who he is. However, he loves Phoebe and wants to support her. Since she believes this group is a good idea, he has agreed to come along although he is a bit sceptical that anything will come from the dialogue sessions.

- Kala, 22, has just started work in a tech company. She did not fit in at school and had few friends. Her transition to senior school was difficult, which caused her to withdraw into the world of fantasy and *anime*. She thrived at university because she found her tribe. She finds social interaction demanding and prefers spending time alone. Kala is nervous about joining such a large group, but was persuaded by Olivia, who felt that Kala had a lot to offer such a group. Kala has benefited from the support she has received and wants to do the same for others.

♦ Amelia, 42, is an HR professional working at the same tech company as Kala. She has developed an interest in neurodiversity and is starting to make changes in the organisation as part of its overall diversity and inclusion initiative. She had been inspired by Olivia and jumped at the chance to join her group. When Amelia realised that Kala was also participating, she reached out to reassure Kala that how she behaved and what she said would be kept confidential by Amelia and would not be reported back to her line manager or find its way onto her employee record. Kala appeared to be comforted by Amelia's words and proactivity.

The context

Olivia had met each person through various gatherings, workshops and webinars that she had either led or participated in and connected with each person both randomly and intentionally. She gauged their interest in wanting to generate more inclusion and belonging in their lives from the chats that she had with each of them. Olivia had the idea that such a diverse group could be powerful in thinking together about how to effect change.

She originally invited 20 people to take part in a series of conversations to explore neuroinclusion. Some were interested but unable to participate in the time frame that Olivia had identified. This left the 13 participants to whom you have been introduced – Limbani, Nathan, Xavier, Phoebe, Myles, Kala, Amelia, Bhavya, Bryn, Finn, Naomi, Rowan and Sofia.

Cultivating love and safety

Olivia spent time with each person individually, to get to know them and share some of her personal history so that she built a strong connection and trust. She invited them to tell her about their experiences with neurodivergence and their reason for signing up for the dialogue group. They also exchanged their hopes and fears for the group. This gave Olivia a sense of how each person might show up in the group and help her prepare for the first session.

Another reason for Olivia building a relationship with each of these characters before convening the group was to gauge their needs and how she could make it inclusive from the start. This included any specific requirements that they had, such as safe foods, specific dietary needs, sensory needs (noise, colours, patterns, quiet spaces, calming objects, etc) and how they liked to process information.

Olivia discovered that Nathan liked to feel that he was in control. Kala, Sofia and Rowan wanted to have information in advance so that they could plan their travel and know what to expect when they arrived at the venue. And she was aware that Finn, like Nathan, was uncomfortable with surprises. The others expressed no specific needs.

Preparing for the first gathering

To cater for these requirements, Olivia provided information to everyone about the:

- purpose of the group, ie the work they were going to do together
- number of sessions the group would have initially, and the dates and times of each one
- venue, which was chosen because of its neuro-affirming approach. This included a short video that showed the outside of the building, the internal layout, the room where they would be meeting, the bathrooms, restaurant and so on, which permitted the participants to familiarise themselves with what to expect
- agenda for the first two sessions and explanation that the group would co-create the schemas of subsequent meetings.

The information was provided in writing (plus the video) and Olivia followed this up with a brief call to which the whole group was invited. This online session started the process of building the connection between each person. This was important because apart from the familial relationships (Nathan/Limbani/Xavier and Phoebe/Myles) and Kala and Amelia being work colleagues, the participants had not met each other.

Bhavya and Naomi were unable to attend this online

briefing, so Olivia asked those present for permission to record the session so that they could listen to the recording before meeting everyone at the first session. Assent was given.

Olivia invited each person to do a brief introduction and state the reason why they wanted to join the group. Then she took them through the information she had provided to explain each point and allow them to ask questions.

The first gathering

Olivia felt it was important to have the dialogue sessions in person as this would permit increased social connection. And now, after weeks of preparation, the day for the first session has arrived.

Arrival

The meeting is scheduled to last a half-day, starting at 10:30 and ending with a late lunch at 14:00 to minimise travelling during rush hours. Olivia arrives at 09:00 to ensure that all the requests she has made have been fulfilled and check the room set-up. The room is spacious. There are plenty of windows to let in natural light. The windows are fitted with blinds to dim any brightness, in case there are any sensitivity issues among the group. There is a circle of chairs in the middle of the room and a couple of sofas and easy chairs against the walls to allow for people to move in and out of the circle. There is a range of fidget toys and other objects that people can use to help them calm down if they feel some discomfort or emotional dysregulation. In addition, Olivia has booked a couple of small rooms so that if anyone needs to take a break they can have some quiet and alone time. She is satisfied with the arrangements and that she has done as much as she can in advance to create the right atmosphere. The rest will happen when the group arrives.

The first person to arrive is Kala. She is wearing noise-cancelling headphones and looks a bit uncomfortable. She speaks quickly and makes brief eye contact as she does so. She chooses a seat in the circle and busies herself taking out her tablet to record notes. Next are Myles and Phoebe. Myles is warm, larger than life, and occupies a big space in the room with his presence. Limbani, Nathan and Xavier follow soon after. They exchange pleasantries with the other members of the group. Xavier spots Kala and makes a beeline for her as she looks to be a similar age to him. She seems relieved to see another young person and visibly relaxes a little.

There is a flurry as Rowan, Finn, Bhavya, Sofia, Amelia and Naomi arrive between 10:10 and 10:25. Bryn sends Olivia a message to say that he is delayed and will be a little late. Olivia greets each person as they arrive and invites them to grab some refreshments. She is a little bit nervous, although the others cannot see this. This is because there are always unknown elements when a new group is forming. She looks around the room at each person and smiles encouragingly at them, as much to settle herself as them. She observes how Nathan and Limbani seem to stick together and not engage much with the other participants. Phoebe and Myles seem used to being at social gatherings together and at ease with moving around the room independently of each other. She's aware that these relationship dynamics might impact the degree of openness and unmasking that each person feels comfortable with. This requires care and attention on her part to foster safety in the group. Olivia had carefully considered this before inviting the family members to participate together and felt on balance that the rewards of having these different voices in the same room outweighed the potential risks.

Olivia is taking in the room and how people are arranged. She notices that Kala is sitting with a tablet on her lap and is looking at it intently. Kala is slightly hunched over and is studiously not making eye contact with anyone. Finn is talking to Naomi, who is sitting on his left while looking straight ahead. Naomi has an interested look on her face and has followed Finn's lead by looking slightly down and ahead. She's leaning slightly towards him. Myles and Nathan are standing by the table that has glasses and bottles of water on it and talking to each other. She sees Nathan laugh at something that Myles has said. Bryn and Rowan are gravitating towards the circle. She overhears them talking about football. Xavier is rummaging through the 'bin' containing the fidget toys. He

> **Relationship dynamics might impact the degree of openness and unmasking that each person feels comfortable with. This requires care and attention on her part to foster safety in the group.**

picks out a fidget cube and shows it to his parents; he has one like it at home. He notices with delight that there are squishy objects, spinners, soft animals of different sizes and textures and bubble wrap gadgets. He selects a couple of stress balls and moves with them in his hands to take a seat next to his mother in the circle. Phoebe, Bhavya and Amelia are standing and are sharing their names and where they have travelled from.

Olivia invites each person to join the circle and make themselves comfortable. There is some toing and froing as each person tends to their needs. Then everyone settles into a seat and the group is ready to start just as the clock approaches 10:36.

Building connection and safety

Personal introductions

Olivia opens the session. She welcomes everyone to the day and thanks them for their willingness to participate. She tells them how excited she is to be embarking on this journey of dialogue with them and that she is curious to see what they will discover along the way. She then invites each person to say a little bit about themselves so that Bhavya and Naomi, who missed the online introductory meeting, can start to bond with the others. Olivia also asks each person to say what their hopes are for participating in this dialogue group. Xavier is a bit squirmy in his seat and is making good use of the stress balls as he speaks haltingly about wanting to do anything that will help others like him. Sofia talks quickly and quietly so that it is hard to hear what she is saying. Bhavya sits upright in her chair and speaks confidently into the circle, looking at no one in particular. Most people look at Olivia as they speak; the exceptions are Kala, who continues to look at her tablet, Amelia, who rests her eyes on each person in the group as she speaks, and Myles, who seems socially confident. He makes funny quips in response to some of the things that people share. These provoke some laughter that releases some of the tension. The atmosphere is one of polite interest.

Icebreakers

Olivia then proposes that the group participates in an icebreaker exercise to help them relax and start talking to each other. She invites them to move around the room and find someone they don't know and speak to each other about one of their hobbies or special interests. The challenge is to keep this to five minutes each, particularly for the group comprising three people.

There is some hesitation as the group absorbs what Olivia has said. She gently encourages them to stand up and move to a space in the room where they can talk and not feel too distracted by the noise of other conversations. Each person chooses the easiest path by deciding to talk to the person sitting next to them. There is a sudden hubbub as people start talking to each other. A couple of the pairs, Kala and Limbani and Sofia and Bryn, move to different corners of the room and sit on a sofa. Olivia sees them smiling and listening to each other intently. She lightly blows her whistle to get their attention and let them know that it is time to swap over. After five minutes she lightly blows her whistle for the second time to end the conversation. It takes a few seconds for the group to quieten down. Olivia invites them to select a different partner/trio and to repeat the exercise, choosing another interest or hobby to talk about. Again, the high energy in the room is palpable as each person talks animatedly to their partner. This time, Olivia lets the conversations run for the full ten minutes with only a verbal reminder halfway through that they should swap over. When ten minutes have elapsed, Olivia lightly blows her whistle and requests that the group pick where they would like to sit in the circle. She tells them that they have the opportunity to select a different seat from the one they originally sat in, if they so choose. However, each person returns to their original seat. Olivia observes that the tension in the group appears to have abated. Everyone's body language seems a little more relaxed.

She then instructs the group on a second exercise, which is to talk about their name. Each person says a little about how they got their name, what it meant, the cultural significance of it, whether they liked it, how others addressed them. Olivia role models this exercise by telling the group about her name. Naomi speaks next, followed by Phoebe and then Limbani. Finn then responds to each of the points she had offered as suggestions for what they might say. Limbani and Bhavya talk about their cultural backgrounds and how their names came from various customs and family traditions. Kala seems more at ease now and talks eloquently about her Sri Lankan heritage. Myles chooses to speak last and again is entertaining. The tales each person tells reveal a little bit of each individual in a safe way. They can share whatever they want with the group. The group hears something about each person's background; even Nathan and Limbani learn new things about each other, which surprises them. Xavier seems a bit dismissive of the exercise. He laughs as he says he didn't know why he had been given his name and that the group should ask his parents. This elicits laughter in the group and a sheepish response from Nathan that he doesn't know why either. Limbani is the one who fills in the gaps.

Norms and ground rules

The group then establishes some norms for how they want to be together and to create a supportive space of safety. There are the typical requests of confidentiality, no question is a stupid one, to listen and not interrupt each other and to be supportive and patient so that if someone is having difficulty framing their thoughts or expressing themself they do not feel pressured. This sparks a request to allow moments of silence and not feel that these need to be filled.

Most contributions come from Amelia, Naomi, Bryn and Nathan. Olivia invites the quieter members to consider their needs and add them if they are not already captured. Sofia states that she needs time to process what is being said so it would be good if there are moments of silence. Olivia requests that each person extends grace to each other, so that if a person says or does something that triggers them, instead of reacting to what they think is meant, the person who finds the situation difficult enquires to better understand what the individual has done rather than rushing to judgement and defensiveness.

Oliva reminds the group that each person is responsible for taking care of their needs. So if they want to move around, stim, go to a quieter space at the edge of the room or take time out, they do that. Her request is that they do this in a way that is respectful to the group. The group seems satisfied with the ground rules they establish and agree to review and adjust them as needed. At this point the group takes a short break.

Concerns and fears

After the break, Olivia asks the group to choose someone they have not yet spoken to and spend some time in pairs (and a trio) discussing their fears for this group. The energy in the room is more sombre and yet everyone seems attentive and engaged. After 20 minutes, Olivia gently brings the group back together and invites them to disclose whatever they are comfortable sharing. The initial admissions are related to the hopes outlined earlier. Olivia notices that no one is expressing their fears and softly encourages them to do so. She reminds them of their ground rule of being vulnerable and courageous. Finn then speaks up, saying that he is concerned about being with a group of strangers for four hours. He explains that he is literal and responds to the content of questions. He finds it difficult to interpret the meaning of words being used or infer what is required from what is not expressed. Kala says that she is the same and worries that she will not be able to follow what the group is saying and therefore make a meaningful contribution. Olivia thanks them both for speaking up. She asks the group how they can accommodate Finn and Kala's tendency for precision. Naomi suggests that each person is prepared to explain what they mean by certain words or phrases if asked, which the group agrees. They request that Kala and Finn and anyone else asks if they are unsure and point to their ground rules of 'patience' and 'no question is too stupid' as being pertinent. They agree to hold each other to account for behaving in accordance with their agreed norms and not rely solely on Olivia to do that for them.

Olivia adds a process ground rule that at moments during

each dialogue, she will invite each person in turn to say what they think while the rest of the group listens silently. She encourages them to imagine that, in these moments, there is a campfire in the middle of the circle and that each person is speaking into the campfire. Everyone else is required to simply listen and hold the space for that person to express and process their thoughts. No one is allowed to interrupt, ask questions or respond to what they hear. When the person finishes speaking they say 'complete'. The group then observes a couple of minutes of silence to allow the words that have been spoken to be internalised by each person before Olivia invites the next contributor to speak. Depending on what emerges, Olivia will judge whether one round in this way is sufficient or that there is more for each individual to share in a second round before moving to a whole group conversation. If, in these later rounds, someone has nothing to add to what they have previously said, they can say so and the next person is called to speak.

Then it is time for a refreshment break. Kala puts her noise-cancelling headphones back on and quickly exits the main room. Xavier sits on the sofa and plays with one of the fidget toys. Rowan joins him on the sofa and Sofia hovers nearby, not quite in their little group. The others mill around the drinks and refreshments station outside their room. Olivia is pleased that they are starting to make connections with each other as this will be important for their dialogue in the coming sessions. Just before the end of the break, Kala returns to the room and Olivia checks on her. She says she's fine but needed some quiet time.

Starting the dialogue

Exploring the language of inclusion

Olivia reminds the group that they can step out of the main circle at any time and move to the sofas or one of the quiet rooms that she's booked. Then she tells them they will start to explore the language of inclusion to generate some sense of how each person interprets words such as *diversity, inclusion, belonging, equity, microaggressions, masking*. Olivia wants to stimulate the group to share their opinions and encourage respectful enquiry about the perspectives being offered. She begins by giving her view of each word, and asks the group to add, subtract, challenge and build on what has been expressed.

There is not much dissent regarding her interpretation of words. However, the exchange becomes more charged as individuals start to share their

> **Human beings form cliques, and that can feel isolating to individuals if they are not part of that group.**

experiences of not being included or feeling that they belonged. Kala chronicles her experience at university of joining a group for her special interest where she immediately felt at home. Others describe some of the microaggressions they have suffered for being different, such as a roll of the eye by others when they spoke or asked questions. The neurodivergent individuals in the group talk about feeling alone, being bullied and so on. Naomi shares her experience of feeling less than the executives she works with because she doesn't have a degree or a high-powered job. She sometimes felt dismissed when she didn't understand the rationale for a particular decision that she had to execute. Limbani speaks about being a Black woman, and how she often wonders whether people were treating her badly because of her race or because they were rude and ignorant towards everyone. Amelia mentions some of the challenges that the leaders in the organisation came to her with. They needed to get the work done and yet they had to accommodate so many different requirements, including mental health issues and being neurodivergent, that they wondered how they could get the performance that they needed without coming unstuck.

As the conversation progresses, each person sees that inclusion and the lack of it affects each of them to some degree in certain settings. Human beings form cliques, and that can feel isolating to individuals if they are not part of that group. More than ever, they see that there is a need for change so that everyone feels welcomed in workspaces and that they are celebrated for their special talents and gifts. This gives them the energy and impetus they need to start the dialogue in earnest.

Listening: the first campfire

At this point, Olivia says that she would like to hear from each person in turn about what is on their mind and how they are feeling in that moment. She asks them to talk into the campfire, which acts as a reminder that each person is going to speak and be heard in silence. Olivia decides for this initial round to speak first to model what she wants from the group. She tells the group that she is grateful for the sunshine as it makes her feel brighter. She is enjoying the energy and engagement of the group. She has a slight headache and is tired. She senses that the group is starting to gel and wonders what is not being expressed. One by one each person shares what is going on for them and how they are feeling.

The general mood is that the group has made a good beginning. A couple of people voice their frustration that the actual dialogue has not yet begun. Olivia notices that Xavier, Rowan and Bryn say little and Bhavya seems distracted. Aside from that there is nothing expressed in the campfire that she feels she needs to pick up with the group. Limbani and Finn have been willing to share deeply personal stories during the gathering, which is a good sign that they have a solid foundation to build on.

> **It is important to take time to form strong bonds and create safety first so that individuals can be fully present and themselves in the group.**

Olivia brings the session to a close by acknowledging the general sentiment in the group and responding to the frustration that has been expressed. She tells them that it is important to take their time to form strong bonds and create safety first so that they can be fully present and themselves in the group. They can take what they learn from how they come together to role model the inclusion that they want to see in other settings, ie that everyone feels seen, heard and cherished for who they are.

Olivia reminds them that lunch is now available and is part of the session. They wander through to the restaurant to a wonderful display of salads, fruit, bread, dips, cheese, biscuits and a selection of hot meals. Olivia checks that all the dietary needs have been met before making her selection from the buffet. They are allocated two tables and seem content to sit together. There are enough people in the group who are socially confident to keep the conversation going at each table while they eat. After 20 minutes or so, people start to depart. Bhavya is the first to leave, closely followed by Kala. The rest disappear in dribs and drabs over the next 15 minutes.

When the last person has left, Olivia goes back to the main room to do a sweep for anything that has been left behind and collect her belongings. She feels a weariness that comes from having put everything into the session. Fortunately, she has a quiet evening ahead of her that will allow her to unwind. She knows that it is important to relax and do her reflections the next day when she is feeling refreshed.

The second gathering

Reconnecting: campfire

Three weeks later, it is time for the second session of the dialogue group. In between the first and second gatherings, Olivia has had conversations with each member of the group. She is pleased to discover that almost everyone is open minded, curious and eager to get going. There is a naïve sense in the group that they can find the solutions to neuroinclusion in a few conversations. Olivia wisely does not dampen their enthusiasm and tries to temper their expectations for the second meeting. She believes that there is still work to be done for individuals to create the loving and compassionate basis for the difficult conversations that lie ahead.

There have been no new requests, so the arrangements and room set-up are the same as before. Everyone seems more comfortable and Olivia has the sense that they are pleased to see each other again. The greetings are warm and even Kala seems to be engaging with the others more than before. Olivia allows everyone to settle and then opens the meeting with a campfire. She requests that each person share their reflections on the first session and how they are feeling about the day. This time she waits to allow someone from the group to speak. Finn goes first. He says that the first session had been different from what he had been expecting and appreciated the time and care that Olivia is taking to first form the love and safety that the group require. He has found the approach refreshing and enjoyed it. Limbani has liked getting to know a little bit about each person and is looking forward to building on that today. She explains that she has a tendency to talk a lot, so likes the campfire technique as a way of balancing the airtime.

Kala and Sofia found the campfire during the first gathering a little scary but also appreciated having the opportunity to voice their thoughts. Xavier says he was concerned that, being the youngest, he didn't have much to contribute to the group. Bryn found himself being transported back in time when he heard some of the stories that people had shared. He recognises these as similar to experiences his brother has had. He is feeling guilty for escaping from home as soon as he could. Bhavya admits that she hasn't reflected on the session because she has been caught up with a project for a new client that she desperately wants to go well.

Amelia has been more aware of instances at work where colleagues have expressed frustration at what they saw as poor quality work without stopping to enquire what might be the underlying cause. She has tried to apply some of the dialogue group's ground rules, such as patience, curiosity and listening without interrupting, to help her colleagues get another perspective on what might be happening. She has had some small breakthroughs with this already.

Naomi says that she had found the campfire empowering and likes the fact that they are not required to respond. She has noticed that she is listening differently to people at work. Myles remains sceptical. He says that the exercises are nice but could not see why they were spending so much time on these. He isn't sure that the group is powerful enough to make a difference. Olivia notices some people shuffling in their seats as they listen to him.

Nathan has been pleasantly surprised. He finds it hard to

engage with people he doesn't know in new settings but has felt quite comfortable with the group. Rowan draws a couple of frames of a cartoon of the group to express how he feels. The first frame shows people in various states of discomfort, such as quaking in their shoes, sweating, teeth chattering. The second frame shows everyone sitting round a campfire toasting marshmallows. He says that he wanted to convey the feeling of bonhomie that he is experiencing.

Once the campfire is complete, Olivia thanks everyone for their contributions and addresses some of the concerns raised. She emphasises that each person has a valid contribution to make and that the group benefits from the diversity that is represented in the room. And she explains that what they are doing is operating on two levels. On one level they are creating a climate of trust and safety for themselves to be able to think together about neuroinclusion. On the second level they are building their own model of neuroinclusion in the group that they can adapt and use in other groups and settings. They have started to get to know each other and learn how to listen respectfully to each other without the need to respond.

After the campfire, they take a 15-minute break, which allows them to reconnect with each other in smaller groupings. Olivia can see that there is a lot of caring for and appreciation of each other being displayed.

Social identity: who's in the room?

After the break, Olivia runs an exercise called 'Who's in the room?' She asks them to stand in a circle. She gives them instructions about the exercise. She will read out some statements. If they want to publicly declare that they identify with the statement, they take a step into the middle of the circle. There is no requirement for them to confirm an identity if they don't want to. Olivia bids them to notice what they experience as each statement is read out, they decide whether or not to step in, and various members of the group step in or are left in the original, outer circle. Before she goes through her list of questions, Olivia requests that they ask for clarification if they are unsure of the meaning but otherwise to perform the exercise in silence. This will allow them to try to identify their responses. She is careful not to ask them to specifically tune into their emotions, since she knows that some members of the group will find this hard to do.

The statements that Olivia reads out start gently, for example, 'Please step in if... you are vegetarian, have a tattoo, are right handed, are an only child, are a middle child, are a parent' and so forth. As the exercise progresses, the statements refer to more risky and less visible identities. 'Please step in if you... identify as male, female, were raised with less than enough money, identify as LGBTQ+, have a learning disability, have been mistreated because of your race, have experienced the effects of alcoholism in your family, have mental health challenges', for instance.

After running through 50 statements, Olivia asks the group to reflect on their experience for a few moments and then requests that they talk about what that had been like for them. People share observations about how the group was a little jokey at the start when the questions were light and low risk but as the statements covered deeper aspects of identity, they noticed varying degrees of vulnerability. It transpires that every person chose not to declare some aspect of their identity during that session because they do not feel ready to disclose that to the group yet. This leads to a fruitful enquiry about what more the group needs to do to increase each person's feeling of safety. Finn asks whether it was reasonable to expect that they would reach the level of safety where everyone feels OK to unmask in such a short time since the group's formation. He believes that everyone masks to some extent in all situations and the group should aim for a level of uncovering that generates new insights and thinking together rather than total unmasking. Olivia recognises this as being true of where the group is today and that this could shift over time in any direction depending on how each person in the group treats everyone else.

Listening: campfire

Olivia requests that each person tell the campfire what they have learnt during the session and what they are going to do to deepen their connection with each other to increase the level of safety in the group. Once the round is complete, Olivia summarises the key themes that have emerged: spend time with at least one other person in the group before the next session, allow moments of silence in the sessions so that the more reflective individuals can process what is happening and encourage each other to speak in addition to the campfire disclosures. She closes the formal part of the gathering and leads them to the restaurant for lunch. Olivia observes that the conversations are flowing more easily than at the first gathering. She sees them performing acts of kindness for each other, making room at the table so they can sit together, pointing out safe foods to Kala and Sofia, and so on.

Once lunch is over, Olivia returns to the main room. She is encouraged by the strengthening of the bonds that she sees in the group. Olivia recognises that the hard work will begin in earnest in the next session as they move into dialogue proper. Olivia needs to manage the complexities of convening a neurodiverse group and explicitly role model the behaviours of listening, respecting, suspending and voicing that are the conditions for dialogue. They have built the foundations for this during their campfire sessions and will take these skills further to be able to respond to each other in a way that honours their own feelings and experiences and values that of the rest of the group. Olivia is feeling both weary and inspired as she wends her way home.

These gatherings establish the foundations for the group to come together subsequently to enter into dialogue about neuroinclusion and think together about how they might foster this in the various groups in which they participate.

Imagine that Olivia continues to take great care in building a safe container for each person both physically and emotionally. This can be witnessed by the varying degrees to which the neurodivergent participants feel able to unmask when they meet. Unmasking takes as many forms as there are neurodivergent individuals, ie it's not possible to always tell if someone feels comfortable to show more of themselves. However, signs may include individuals asking for help to do things that come easily to others, slowing down their speed of speaking or being open about what they need. Olivia made sure to check in with each person in between gatherings and at various times during the gatherings to see what they required. Her role modelling set the example for the others.

Olivia opens the third gathering and subsequent ones by reconnecting via a campfire (as they did in the second gathering). In the third coming-together, Olivia then invites them to begin the exploration of neuroinclusion. She opens the space for anyone to start speaking about neuroinclusion, what it evokes for them, how they relate to the word, the meaning they give it. She encourages them to free-associate and say whatever comes up for them. She requests that everyone tune into themselves to notice what is happening for them as they listen or speak, the sensations they experience in their bodies, how they feel, and to be curious about that. This is not a campfire, so anyone can but no one needs to speak; silences are welcomed into the space. The purpose of the dialogue is to have a conversation in which they can learn through the process of the group. There is no defined outcome, which gives the group freedom to express what they want without the pressure of coming up with a solution. In this third gathering and subsequent ones, Olivia allows 30 minutes for a closing campfire so that each person can say whatever they want to close the dialogue for that day.

Over time, this dialogue group builds a strong connection and feeling of safety with each other. That does not mean that everyone feels safe to unmask all the time or express ideas which others may find confronting or challenging. There are moments when each person holds back for various reasons

– this is no silver bullet. However, they each feel enriched by the dialogue and leave with ideas about what they can do to foster more neuroinclusion. The group experiments with various formats of meeting, for example virtually with videos on or off, or being outside in nature.

One aspect Olivia thinks a lot about is ending. The group will come to a point where it is no longer serving a useful purpose and it is vital to end well. This is something that Olivia is tuning into during every gathering and will check in with the group to involve them in the decision to close the group and determine how they want to do that.

The schematic opposite shows the key phases in the dialogue process that Olivia facilitated.

I mentioned earlier that the scenario depicted was one way of bringing to life the four elements of love, safety, social identity and dialogue in my model for neuroinclusion (see Chapter 3). It requires time and patience to foster an environment in which a diverse group can come together in dialogue to think together. I have not portrayed the dialogue that the characters went on to have about neuroinclusion because dialogue is emergent and depends on the characters who take part. There is no 'one size fits all' solution and the ideas that they will have formulated will have emerged from them feeling safe to share their inner thoughts, experiences and stories, listening deeply to what was being spoken and what was left unsaid, reflecting on the overall story that was developing from the group and thinking together about what that meant for neuroinclusion. I believe that neuroinclusion comes when we feel safe to connect with ourselves and others in an honest and open way with courage, compassion and wisdom in any setting to build those four pillars in any social setting.

In the final chapter, I explore how Olivia's techniques can be adapted for work environments.

OLIVIA'S PROCESS FOR CREATING A DIALOGUE

BEFORE THE GATHERING

STEP 1: PURPOSE OF DIALOGUE
- Define the reason for the dialogue
- Determine who should participate

STEP 3: BUILDING RAPPORT
- Meet each individual 1:1
- Getting to know each other
- Understanding needs

DURING THE GATHERING

STEP 5: CREATE A WELCOMING SPACE
- Zones in the main room
- Sensory needs
- Quiet spaces
- Equipment (fidget toys, exercises)

STEP 7: LEARNING THE ART OF DIALOGUE
- Discussion on low stakes topic related to purpose of the dialogue
- Role-modelling key skills of listening and voicing

POST GATHERING

STEP 9: INDIVIDUAL CONNECTIONS
- Check-in with each individual 1:1
- Understanding needs for next gathering

STEP 2: DESIGN
- Develop outline of proposed programme (no. of sessions, focus of each session, timeline etc.)
- Create detailed design of the first gathering (meeting)

STEP 4: PREPARE FOR FIRST GATHERING
- Selection of venue (ensure caters for identified needs)
- Brief participants (written and verbal info - agenda & timing, video of venue, Q&A)

STEP 6: BUILDING CONNECTION & SAFETY
- Introductions & icebreakers
- Norms & ground rules
- Hopes & fears

STEP 8: CLOSING THE GATHERING
- Campfire technique
- Acknowledge what has been said
- Summarise the key moments
- Signpost next steps

(Repeat steps 5-9 for each subsequent gathering)

Part 3

Chapter 5

Generating neuroinclusion in work environments

In this chapter, I want to focus on neuroinclusion at work. The reason is that outside work, neurodivergent people more easily find their tribe (the people who understand them and they can be themselves with) because they can exert more choice regarding who they spend their time with. At work, employees, neurodivergent and neurotypical alike, have little control over who their work colleagues are (unless they are the boss). They may find it difficult to work well together if they do not understand what makes each person tick and their strengths, vulnerabilities and challenges. So, generating neuroinclusive spaces at work is where I see the biggest need and potential gain.

Let's unpick what Olivia did with her group to identify what leaders and colleagues can do to engender neuroinclusive workspaces.

Cultivate trust with each individual

Olivia spent time with each individual to build a relationship with them, understand their hopes, fears, needs. In a work environment it is vital that someone takes the time to do that. Ideally, it will be the leader of the team, who is not necessarily the line manager, since colleagues come together in various groupings to perform tasks. The leader needs to be at the forefront in fostering neuroinclusion. This starts by them getting to know their team members on an individual basis.

> **Outside work, neurodivergent people more easily find their tribe (the people who understand them and they can be themselves with) because they can exert more choice regarding who they spend their time with.**

In my experience, leaders establish a cadence of individual meetings to check in with each person regarding their work. Some also invite their team members to talk about more personal matters. I believe that if the leader is to create neuroinclusion, they need to establish conversations that are focused on forming a good connection between them and their team members. I would go so far as to say that the leader's most important task is to create an authentic connection with each person in their team in which they role model vulnerability. They do this by harnessing their Three Companions – courage, compassion and wisdom – to reveal who they are, their gifts, struggles and what support they need. By doing so they create an environment that encourages each person in their team to do the same.

As we saw with Olivia, building trust comes with time. According to David Maister, Charles Green and Robert Galford (2021), trustworthiness increases with credibility, reliability and intimacy and decreases with self-interest. Intimacy comes from both parties sharing personal details about themselves and finding points of connection, whether that is similar backgrounds, family, passions, pastimes or spirituality, for example. Credibility is derived from having the knowledge and expertise required to perform the role. This works both ways as the leader needs to feel that the team member has the requisite skills to function well. Reliability is about keeping your promises. It's about doing what you say you will do on time and honouring your commitments.

I would go so far as to say that the leader's most important task is to create an authentic connection with each person in their team in which they role model vulnerability.

When dealing with neurodivergent individuals, care needs to be taken in defining expectations. Often leaders assess performance based on *what* is achieved (outcomes) and *how* that result has been accomplished, ie the way the individual engages with others to get things done. While I have been a proponent of this approach in the past, I realise now that this does not take into account that some neurodivergent people often get into trouble at work because their social interactions do not meet neurotypical standards. I think this comes from a lack of understanding or willingness of the complainants to see beyond the communication difficulties that some of their neurodivergent peers experience. If the leader forms an intimate connection with each team member, they can manage the expectations of the people they need to interact with by explaining the specific needs each person in the team has and developing workarounds. For example, a neurodivergent person may be experiencing burnout and be less able to perform tasks than usual. By informing their colleagues, the leader can work with them to find solutions, particularly if there are time-sensitive tasks, such as using temporary labour to fill in the gaps.

It is easy to make assumptions that a neurodivergent person is not committed, is being lazy or doesn't care if they are continually late for meetings, miss deadlines or appear unable to follow what seem like simple instructions. It is important that the line manager asks their team member what is going on and is open to the answer rather than dismissing it as an excuse. If the line manager is neurodivergent themselves, this comprehension will come more easily.

If an individual only considers their own needs, desires, goals, etc, it will be hard to build trust with them because you believe that they will only do something if it furthers their agenda. Consider the different feeling that is engendered from the same act but different motives. For example, your leader may agree to you working from home one day per week because they see that you are more productive, so they can demand more of you. Contrast this with the leader who understands that you get overwhelmed by too much noise and busyness in the office and it's good for your wellbeing to work from home. You will sense the genuineness of the leader's concern for you from what they say and do, which will engender loyalty and a willingness to go the extra mile for that person. If you detect that the leader's primary concern is about achieving results, you may feel wary and more guarded, which will hamper your ability to perform – they will get the opposite result of what they were aiming for.

Form team bonds and norms

Having built some understanding at the individual level, when the leader brings the team together they can start to create an inclusive environment by taking time to build some team cohesion.

Offsites, such as the sessions that Olivia ran, are wonderful opportunities to do this because they take the team out of their normal working environment to be together without the constraints of the daily grind of getting the job done. Offsites are deliberately designed to inspire and invigorate team members, to allow them to unwind, get to know each other outside their professional roles and forge stronger bonds between team members. Done thoughtfully, they can set the tone for how the team will work together. I strongly encourage team leaders to create this space early in the team's genesis as this can help to establish the love, safety and connection that is required for neuroinclusion that will result in superior team working. This shift from 'business as usual' can be signalled by physically meeting in a different location from where the team usually meets or ensuring that the style and content of the meeting is distinct from usual.

However, these offsite events can create significant stress

for neurodivergent staff – navigating a different travel route, new venue/environment, the expectation to interact with colleagues for an extended period. Olivia took great care to prepare her participants for this through her meticulous planning, including starting mid-morning to minimise travel during rush hour, and her communication. Organisers of offsite events should aim for this level of care so that everyone can arrive on an equal footing.

Offsites are a special form of gathering. Work meetings can also be used to create neuroinclusion in how they are conducted.

You may remember that Olivia spent time establishing group norms. I believe that it is important to do this explicitly for teams. If the team leader is not intentional, implicit norms will still emerge, which may or may not match the expectations of the team leader and members. A potential issue with permitting implicit norms for how the team behaves is that not everyone in the team will understand what these are. For example, if the team meeting is due to start at 10:00 and finish at 11:30, an autistic team member will take that literally and turn up on time or a little early to be ready to start at 10:00 and expect to leave at 11:30. Other members of the team will join at 10:00 but not be quite ready to engage, because they haven't had a break after their previous meeting. One or two participants will believe it's OK to arrive late because their previous meeting overran. The leader or chair of the meeting often delays the actual start time to allow everyone to be present or permits interruptions as people join late. This can seem perplexing and/or unfair to the autistic person. It can seem that there is an unwritten rule that it is OK to waste others' time.

Establishing unambiguous ground rules is an opportunity for each individual to say what they need from others. When the team is in the early stages of forming, members will be reticent about sharing anything profound. The leader may need to encourage openness since individuals may be more concerned with fitting in than being honest about what will enable them to work well with other team members. The leader can do this by declaring some things that they need, for example people speaking one at a time or choosing backgrounds in virtual meetings that are not distracting. This will encourage others to state their needs.

It is important for the leader to regularly review the norms with the team in a meaningful way. This means having an in-depth conversation about every rule and each person's experience of how well the norm supports them and the team to perform at their best. The leader needs to be genuine in their desire and probe to get beyond surface-level comments such as active participation in team discussions to establish and reinforce norms that support neuroinclusion.

Two ground rules that I have found useful when leading teams or facilitating groups are adapted from *The Skilled Facilitator* by Roger Schwarz (2002). These are:

1. test assumptions and inferences
2. use specific examples and agree on what important words mean.

Test assumptions and inferences

As I mentioned earlier, in conversations we make inferences based on what we see and hear and then act on that conclusion. Similarly, we act as though assumptions are true. This can lead to miscommunication and misunderstandings between people.

For example, if someone is not participating in a meeting or they have their camera off during a virtual meeting, someone may assume that they are not interested, bored, doing something else and so forth. This could lead to their being excluded from further discussions. This is often the situation faced by neurodivergent people who may find it difficult to know when to insert themselves into the conversation, feel that they have nothing valuable to say or find it hard to think on their feet even when they know the subject well.

To listen and respond effectively, we need to develop self-awareness about the inferences we are making in the moment so that we can test these out in real time rather than conclude that they are true and act based on that. Returning to the ladder of inference, the diagram opposite outlines the steps we can take to notice what is happening in the moment and choose how to respond.

You will notice that for each rung on the ladder of inference, there are questions that we can pose to ourselves to interrupt our tendency to make assumptions about what is happening in a meeting and act as though these are true.

Double empathy is a related issue that arises in miscommunication between autistic and allistic (non-autistic) people. I like to pride myself that I am open to people having a different perspective from mine and that I can learn from that. However, there are times when I believe my way of viewing a situation is right. There is only one answer, *can't you see that?*

THE LADDER OF INFERENCE

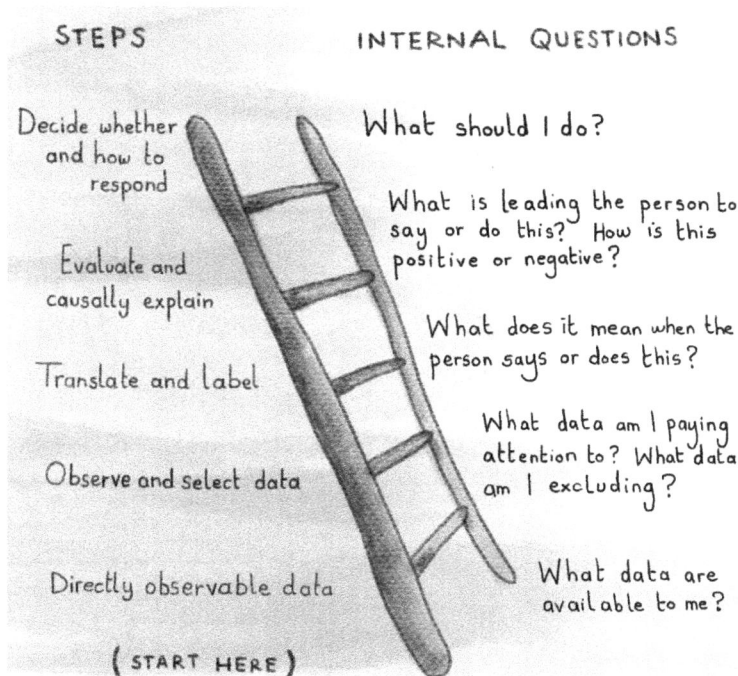

STEPS

INTERNAL QUESTIONS

Decide whether and how to respond

What should I do?

What is leading the person to say or do this? How is this positive or negative?

Evaluate and causally explain

What does it mean when the person says or does this?

Translate and label

What data am I paying attention to? What data am I excluding?

Observe and select data

Directly observable data

What data are available to me?

(START HERE)

This was beautifully illustrated by a neurodivergent client and friend. He wrote a letter on a piece of paper, tilted the paper so that I could see it, and asked me what the letter was. I said 'p'. He responded, 'It's not "p", it's "d".' To which I replied, that's because you are looking at it from a different perspective. His response was, 'The right answer is that this is a "d".'

I was left with a feeling that *it depends*, which I thought was very liberal of me. In fact, I was feeling smug until I understood the point he was making. This was that when neurotypical and neurodivergent people see things differently, the expectation is that the neurodivergent individual needs to do the work to change their perspective.

The theory of double empathy is that when people with different experiences of the world interact, they will struggle to empathise with each other. This issue becomes exacerbated with differences in communication styles and use of language. Generally, allistic people believe that the problem stems from the autistic person. However, the theory suggests that the double empathy problem arises due to a lack of reciprocity and mutual understanding.

> **When neurotypical and neurodivergent people see things differently, the expectation is that the neurodivergent individual needs to do the work to change their perspective.**

If we test our assumptions and inferences, we are more likely to pause and reflect before choosing to respond to what we see and hear.

Use specific examples and agree on what important words mean

Using specific examples and agreeing on what important words mean is important to create a shared understanding of what is being said and generate a common base of data. Often in meetings, people talk in general terms, and it is not always clear to everyone present what is being discussed.

Specific examples use directly observable data to name people, places, things or events. When someone provides a specific example, it brings what they are saying to life and we can better understand the point and meaning.

I frequently encounter the phenomenon of everyday words being given a different interpretation to what is intended. For example, *adaptability* is often interpreted as being related to change and being flexible. However, in some situations, the speaker is referring more specifically to one's ability to adapt their ways of communicating and engaging with others, for example with different needs for information, big picture vs detail, direct vs finesse.

> **Specific examples help people agree on what important words mean.**

Specific examples help people agree on what important words mean.

In addition to meeting norms, there are rules about a range of issues such as core hours, place of work, how performance is measured. These expectations are often built on what works for most neurotypical people, even if they don't like it – for example, working from home versus going into the office. Organisations have mandated that their employees return to working in the office because that improves connection and creativity. While that may be true, not everyone can function well in a noisy, busy environment. Being inclusive means considering how to accommodate the needs of all team members. These are not easy questions to answer. Courage, compassion and wisdom can help us have the right mindset to engage in dialogue to think together about these issues.

Know yourself

The purpose of forming strong bonds among team members is so that individuals feel that they are valued for who they are and have a sense of belonging. When we feel we belong, we feel safe to show more of ourselves. This is important because when we cover up who we are (masking) or change our behaviours to fit in with the majority (code switching) it takes energy that we could be using more productively.

My belief is that by role-modelling willingness to do the inner work to know themselves better, team leaders encourage their team members to do the same. Providing opportunities for them to reflect individually and as a team is rare in organisations and so valuable because individuals can deepen their self-insight. They can learn how they contribute to the group cohesion (or lack of) when they are being triggered by something related to their past and when their reaction is because of what is happening in a team dynamic.

> **Leaders need to start where each person is and understand what they are willing to and can do.**

A note of caution: it is crucial not to force people to do reflection if that is not what they want to do. Leaders need to start where each person is and understand what they are willing to and can do. For example, being asked to reflect may not be helpful for someone with ADHD, whose brain is constantly firing, and they may have a voice in their head giving a continuous commentary on what they should say or do. The leader needs to consider that neuroinclusion means designing with everyone in mind and not forcing a one-size-fits-all approach to creating neuroinclusion. That would be ironic.

One approach to forming these connections is by exploring the various social identities that each person has and is willing to share. Olivia started this process with the 'name' exercise in the first session. I usually find that people really enjoy talking about their name. It starts to bust some myths and assumptions that team members are holding about their colleagues.

Olivia built on this with the 'Who's in the room?' exercise. It is a powerful exercise that can initiate a different type of conversation in the team because they are prompted to think about their social identities in ways that they have not done before. It makes them more explicit. What I like about this exercise is that unless someone in the group knows you extremely well, you are free to publicly declare or withhold some of your social identities. I remember facilitating this exercise and feeling shocked that most participants stepped inside the circle when I said, 'Step in if you have had any addictions.' I was surprised that they were so open about this. It took me some time to realise that my own interpretation of addiction was related to drugs and alcohol, whereas it could be anything. The people stepping into the circle were not saying that they were alcoholics or drug addicts. My interpretation came from being married to two alcoholics and still feeling shame about that. This illustrates to me that it is important to notice our bias towards various identities and how that influences how we relate to them. Having had first-hand experiences of living with alcoholics, I am more compassionate towards them and their family members, and yet it still takes bravado for me to admit my own history with alcoholism publicly.

The identity wheel (see Creating neuroinclusive spaces: social identity) is a powerful tool for team members to gain deeper insights about their peers. This exercise can go deep depending on what people want to reveal, so it's important to ensure that there is already a good level of trust and safety in the team.

Each person is required to do some pre-work to create their own identity wheel.

Having reflected on their identity wheels individually, the team members come together to tell their stories. Each person takes a turn to talk about each aspect of their social identity. They can share whatever they feel comfortable with sharing. As each person takes a turn, everyone else listens in silence.

It is profound because at work we tend to share more surface-level aspects of our identity – mother, father, partner, profession, where we live/grew up, etc – but maybe no one at work knows about any personal tragedies we've experienced or what it's like not to find your nationality on forms asking for demographic data. Learning more about ourselves and others allows us to be more patient and understanding of quirks, habits, communication styles and so on that hitherto irritated us because we now know what is behind them. For example, if a neurodivergent person asks a lot of questions, it's because they need the clarity of what is expected.

Generate awareness

The line manager can use the concepts of dialogue to have these meetings with their team members. Having built the foundations of love, trust and safety, the team can gently explore their relationships with each person so that each has an understanding of their effect on the other. For example, a team leader may know that their team member finds it difficult to follow standard operating procedures. It takes them weeks to learn and retain information that only takes two or three days for most of their colleagues. How do they balance patience and caring so that they do not add undue pressure with getting the level of performance that is required to hit the team's targets?

Engaging in dialogue can help both sides gain new perspectives and to think together about how to solve this dilemma. These are difficult conversations to have because each person can become entrenched in their view of the situation and feel that the other person is the problem.

Our Three Companions – courage, compassion and wisdom – can help us be in the mindset to create the best environment for this kind of conversation to occur since it requires each person to give and receive feedback about the impact each has on the other in a spirit of being curious, open and wanting to learn. This happens when there is love and safety in the relationship.

Team dialogue

Having built the foundations to generate love among team members, built psychological safety and gained insight into 'who's in the room', the stage is set to engage in dialogue. Dialogue in this context is about thinking together about issues that impact the team and the team's work. I have outlined the key elements that Isaacs identified as necessary conditions for dialogue, namely listening, respecting, suspending and voicing. How can we turn this into something practical that can be done at work? Nancy Kline's work on thinking environments is a good place to start (Kline 1999).

A thinking environment allows individuals to think for themselves and think well with others. There are ten components to creating a thinking environment:

1. attention – listening with respect, interest and fascination
2. incisive questions – removing assumptions that limit ideas
3. equality – treating each other as thinking peers
4. appreciation – practising a 5:1 ratio of appreciation to criticism
5. ease – offering freedom from rush or urgency
6. encouragement – moving beyond competition
7. feelings – allowing sufficient emotional release to restore thinking
8. information – providing a full and accurate picture of reality
9. place – creating a physical thinking environment that says back to people, 'You matter'
10. diversity – adding quality because of the differences between us.

1. Attention

This is listening without interruption. One of the beauties of coaching is that the coach provides a reflective space for their client to think. Many of the elements listed above that create a thinking environment are present in a coaching session. Learning to hold silence is one of the most difficult and most powerful skills that a coach needs to learn. Novice coaches often get caught up in the loop of feeling that they need to be seen to add value, they need to be seen to be actively listening, asking intelligent questions and guiding their clients towards a solution. Learning to let go of this need and being more present with their clients allows the latter to do their own work. Clients are the experts in their situation and if we allow them, they will find the requisite answers.

This phenomenon is also true in other work settings. As Nancy Kline wrote eloquently, 'The quality of your attention determines the quality of the other person's thinking.'

In some of my interviews, my interlocutors were surprised at what they shared. Giving them the space and time to talk about something that was important to them and being listened to allowed them to surface memories and discuss things that made them feel validated. Experiencing this was special and humbling for me.

Creating a thinking environment for someone else means that we have to be comfortable with sitting in silence and listening. We need to provide space for the other person and not rush in the first moment that we can when they stop speaking. There is usually more for them to think and say and if we quickly interject to ask a question or share our thoughts, we disturb their thinking and processing of their situation. We interrupt their ability to generate insights and solutions. Even when the individual seems to be looking to us for answers, we can hold out in silence, which gives them the space to think more deeply. When we have waited for what feels like an uncomfortably long time, we can then ask open questions that invite the person to think further: 'What else comes to mind?' 'What else are you thinking about this?'

Knowing that they are not going to be cut off allows them to think well. Having their own thoughts and saying them out loud is part of an internal process that unlocks new thoughts and ideas. When we remain quiet and give the other person space to think and sort out what is happening to and for them, it can feel like we have done nothing; however, for the 'speaker' it has been an invaluably rich gift of time and space for reflection.

In the West, we commonly believe that we demonstrate we are being attentive by making eye contact. This is not universally true; for example, in some Eastern cultures it can be seen as a sign of aggression or disrespect. And, as I mentioned before, for some neurodivergent people, particularly those who are autistic, making eye contact is uncomfortable. It's important not to assume that our way is the only way of showing respectful attention. Opening a conversation by exploring what respectful attention looks like for the other person and adopting that practice demonstrates that you value the individual.

2. Incisive questions

These are designed to remove limiting beliefs and assumptions. If someone seems to be stuck, we can ask them what they are assuming that might be holding them back. Replace that limiting belief with a positive freeing one (the opposite of what they believe) in an incisive question. This will unfreeze them. For instance, a manager may want to be more inclusive by opening up work opportunities for everyone but get stuck on how to do that because they believe that for a specific role the person needs to be co-located on the same site as the team. Having uncovered this assumption, the incisive question would be, 'If this role did not need to be co-located on the same site as the team, how would you approach the recruitment?'

Finding good questions is an important aspect of dialogue. These are questions for which we do not know the answer rather than statements or judgements in disguise. I find myself in dialogue with myself as I write this book, asking questions that I do not know the answer to. Such as, 'Am I being too simplistic? Am I the right person to be doing this? Will my interviewees find what I have to say of value or will they be disappointed? What are humans capable of? How can I ensure that my ideas are truly inclusive?' And I am suspending my need to answer these questions as I continue my exploration of the ideas that are forming in my mind from what I have learnt.

3. Equality

In a thinking environment, everyone is treated equally irrespective of the hierarchy. Each person gets a turn at speaking. Knowing this increases the quality of attention that each person gives as they want to ensure that they are able to take into account what has gone before. There is the possibility of wanting to look clever or being afraid of sharing honestly what one is thinking if it goes against the majority view. So it is important for the convenor to establish and reinforce clear ground rules that the space is not for point scoring but for sharing one's truth about the topic. Olivia did this on a few occasions, including reminding the group that all contributions were valued, establishing norms with the group and introducing campfires.

4. Appreciation

Letting the speaker know specifically how they are appreciated increases the quality of their thinking. Appreciation needs to be genuine and concrete. So it's important to notice something good and to say it sincerely. It is also being gracious to receive the admiration as it is, even if you don't feel that it's true. Humility is about knowing our strengths and limitations and neither elevating our strengths nor falsely playing them down. The compliment that the other person has given you is how they perceive you. To demur and deny this is a form of rejection, which could feel hurtful to the giver of the praise. Rejection sensitivity dysphoria (RSD) is a common trait among people with ADHD. RSD is characterised by emotional pain and dysregulation that is triggered by perceived rejection, criticism or failure. The trigger can seem insignificant to someone else, such as being teased for being late for a meeting, being spoken over, not given time to express their ideas, their ideas being challenged. The best response you can give to a compliment is a simple 'thank you' and take in what has been said.

5. Ease

Being at ease in the presence of someone who is trying to think helps them to relax and that stimulates them to generate ideas. One way of showing ease is to slow down the pace in the meeting from the normal frenetic speed of the working day. The facilitator of the session can create spaciousness by the pace at which they speak, their tone of voice and allowing pauses and silences. The invitation to each speaker is to take their time and express all that they are thinking about the topic. When they have finished speaking, the facilitator can pause and allow silence before asking what else they are thinking about the topic. Slowing down permits individuals to access deeper knowing, thoughts and ideas, while urgency creates pressure, which can destroy quality thinking.

6. Encouragement

Encouragement is about giving others the courage to dream and explore new frontiers in thinking by eliminating competition between thinkers. Often we believe that we need to have a fully formed thought or idea before we articulate it. In a thinking environment, if we feel supported to explore and are given an opportunity to think out loud, this is not the case.

This suits my personality type because I am an extrovert, so this is my natural way of thinking.

When we feel in competition with others, wanting to show that we are smarter or more creative than them, this mindset limits our capacity to pursue our thoughts and ideas fully. For example, I have wanted to impress someone whom I held in high esteem by asking them a smart question that showed I was thinking well. My energy was focused on being clever rather than allowing myself to examine the concepts they were presenting from different angles. Similarly, if the thinker feels that others are adversaries, they will be more focused on the potential threat than on thinking.

While we all sense danger at times, for neurodivergent people this state is heightened and they expend significant energy trying to say and do the 'right' things. Thinking out loud may feel unsafe, particularly when you have been labelled weird or difficult most of your life for the ideas that you express. Promoting an environment where everyone feels encouraged to think deeply rather than threatened or in competition with others creates a space for different thinking.

7. Feelings

How someone feels about a topic is valuable information that can help the team to gain new perspectives that they have not seen before. But we're not supposed to show our emotions at work. There's still a prevailing view that this is unprofessional! We get embarrassed when someone starts to cry at work and so do they. However, crying, venting or expressing our emotions in some way is often a release for us. Rather than becoming incapacitated, we are often unblocked and can think more clearly than before about the issue at hand. So holding a respectful space for someone to feel their emotions is extremely valuable and can lead to powerful learning for the individual. *Why are they feeling that way? What does the emotion signify?*

That said, it can be challenging to witness strong emotions – anger, for instance. For someone who is neurodivergent, this can be hard, especially if it's directed at them, as it can be experienced as a perceived threat. However, it is best to allow the person with the strong emotions to voice what they are feeling and to fully listen in a calm manner with equanimity. The role of the facilitator is key here since they can bear witness not only to the person who is expressing their feelings but also the effect on the rest of the group. At an appropriate time, the facilitator can support each person to state what that impact has been for them. It takes skill to ensure that space is given for each person to express their feelings without fear of judgement or invalidation.

8. Information

When we typically listen, we are often thinking about our reply to what is being said, ie sharing information that supports our position or asking questions that require the speaker to justify their thoughts. In a thinking environment it is important not to interrupt the individual. If we ask for information that disturbs the speaker's flow, we disrupt their contemplation. Conversely, if we allow room for the individual to share their thoughts, it can lead to us gleaning some valuable information about a situation that we didn't know. Rather than succumb to our desire for information, we need to closely observe what is happening so that we notice if the person is actively thinking. For some neurodivergent people, it can be hard to see whether they are cogitating. I work with someone whose inner voice is constantly asking questions, taking their thoughts off at a tangent and challenging their thoughts because they are not logical – for example, both exploring a metaphor and observing that it didn't make sense literally. I have learnt to be quiet so that he can notice this inner conversation, determine how well it is serving him in the moment and then respond to my question. Establishing some tools and techniques that support individuals to honour each person's thinking time is important. Exploring approaches openly at the start of the session can go a long way to enabling each person's needs to be considered.

9. Place

The original formulation of the components of a thinking environment was for an in-person meeting and so considering the physical space was important. Since Covid-19, we have moved to more online or hybrid meetings, so we need to extend this component to address virtual meetings. The thinking environment should communicate to the participants that they matter. To do this well requires asking them what they need and want in the space. This would take into account sensory and processing needs. For an in-person meeting, the physical space could include different areas that invite movement, objects that can be used for stimming and consideration given to the use of colours, textures, textiles, noise etc. We saw this in the vignette, where Olivia took care in choosing an environment that allowed for various needs. In a virtual environment, each person can control their own space; however, there may be sensitivities related to being online and looking at a screen for prolonged periods. The convenor can allow for this by inviting each person to take care of their needs, for example camera on or off, asking for/ taking breaks as required, joining breakout rooms or not.

10. Diversity

In groups, diversity enhances thinking because it allows for different viewpoints and experiences. Organisations are realising the value of having diverse teams that represent their customer base and therefore can bring the customers' perspectives into team discussions. The thinking environment challenges two limiting assumptions that are prevalent in our society:

- the dominant group is superior so everyone should think like them, and
- because the dominant group is superior it should have power over the others.

Participants can identify many groups that they belong to in which they have experienced societal prejudice or discrimination. Inviting them to write down the limiting assumptions that society has about each group and then creating an incisive question to remove each of these, as a group, can enable the group to gain insight into each other's experience of fighting internalised oppression. This can help neurotypical people to understand this from the perspective of being neurodivergent, and for neurodivergent people to see what it might be like to be marginalised due to other aspects of social identity.

Our prejudices about the ability of others to think will impact the quality of our listening and attention. I think society has instilled in many neurodivergent people the belief that they are stupid because they struggle with some things that are regarded as ordinary for and by neurotypical people. This can inhibit neurodivergent people in doing their best thinking. So it's important that we truly value what each person brings to a group and the thinking environment.

As I have been contemplating ideas for creating neuroinclusion, I have challenged my default approach of facilitating learning. For example, to enable someone to go deeper, I often ask them about their emotions and somatic experiences.[7] However, for many neurodivergent people this can be problematic because they have alexithymia (a trait in which individuals have difficulty in identifying, understanding or expressing their emotions – it can be regarded as emotional blindness) or they have suffered trauma that means that exploring their sensations does not feel safe. It was an interesting revelation for me. As I pondered further, I remembered that I had successfully supported some neurodivergent individuals to identify and name their emotions by using tools such as emotion cards and written definitions to see what resonated with their

---

7 Somatic experiences refer to those that affect the body.

experience. The insight that came from this contemplation was to offer different ways of helping individuals to think and not to limit my approaches by presupposing that someone does not have the capacity to do what I'm asking. Being aware of our preconceptions allows us to challenge and interrupt them with incisive questions.

If we return to what Olivia did in our vignette, you can see that she implemented many elements of the thinking environment to create the right climate for the dialogue on neuroinclusion. She convened a diverse group that came from different walks of life, experiences and cultures. She ensured that there was spaciousness by not filling the agenda with many topics. She reinforced equality by reassuring Xavier that his contribution was as valuable as those of older participants with more life experience. Olivia ensured that everyone had an opportunity to speak without interruption at key moments through the campfire technique. She took considerable care in identifying and responding to the needs of each person in the information that she shared and the choice and set-up of the venue. And she started with some exercises that set a positive tone – talking about their interests or hobbies and their hopes.

I trust you can see that there is a strong overlap between these components and what we have explored earlier in Chapter 3 describing the four elements for dialogue – listening, respecting, suspending and voicing.

Conclusion

If you have read this book expecting me to wave a magic wand and give you the answer, then you may be feeling disappointed. Neuroinclusion is a complex topic and not one for which there is a simple solution. I believe that neuroinclusion is more a way of being and a guiding philosophy than an end in itself.

> **Neuroinclusion is more a way of being and a guiding philosophy than an end in itself.**

The purpose of creating neuroinclusive spaces is to provide the conditions for each person in a team or organisation to thrive. To thrive we need to feel valued for who we are, as we are, with all our idiosyncrasies. And when we thrive we can accomplish outstanding things individually and as a team.

To foster neuroinclusion we need to love each other (accept and cherish each person), create psychological safety, and understand how our social identities affect how we feel in different situations. This base sets the stage for having dialogue. When we embrace deep listening, respecting, suspending and voicing we generate new insights that emerge from being open and curious to learn about ourselves and other participants in the dialogue. With these new perspectives the team can learn to think together about various topics that can lead to significant change. Employing the components of the thinking environment can provide a practical way into dialogue.

Underpinning all of these are our Three Companions of courage, compassion and wisdom, which enable us to be alive to the suffering of others and want to alleviate that, have the fortitude to look at ourselves and face some difficult aspects of who we are and where that has originated, and the ability to know what to say or do at key moments.

> **I believe it takes effort by everyone, neurotypical and neurodivergent alike, to generate neuroinclusive spaces in which we can all flourish.**

This book is called *Wired Differently, Understood Together* because I believe it takes effort by everyone, neurotypical and neurodivergent alike, to generate neuroinclusive spaces in which we can all flourish. Throughout this book, I have chosen to highlight some of the difficulties that many neurodivergent people face because these are less well known and diminished. From my interactions with the neurodivergent people I have met, they can and do show courage, compassion and wisdom towards others. I have heard about people who struggle to express these qualities but this doesn't mean that they don't possess them.

I believe that as human beings we all deserve to feel that we belong and are received for who we are and that any and every thing we can do to give that feeling to another person is worth the endeavour.

Epilogue

A little over a year after the painful experience I described in the Prologue, I am supporting neurodivergent people in ways that enable them to feel safe to explore topics that are important to them and to make significant progress in their ability to navigate people, spaces and topics that they had previously found distressing. They have new-found confidence that they can handle

I believe that as human beings we all deserve to feel that we belong and are received for who we are and that any and every thing we can do to give that feeling to another person is worth the endeavour.

more of the challenges that life throws at them.

I am growing significantly too, as I learn to see the world differently from my interactions with them. I feel deeply honoured and grateful that they trust me to support them. I am in awe of the courage they show to keep striving and wanting to succeed in a world that works against them in many ways. And I have the humility to know that I have experienced only a microcosm of the rich tapestry of life that I have been missing until now.

This journey began with that awakening. Since I was able to draw on my Three Companions, I was able to go through that difficult experience and come out stronger. This was because I was willing to face an uncomfortable truth about myself and have the self-compassion that increased my determination to be a better person.

Thank you to those of you who were willing to give me this chance. I have immense gratitude to you for the gift you have given me.

Wired Differently, Understood Together

(a poem)

Throw a stone into water and it creates a ripple
that spreads further than the individual who threw it.
But one stone might only drop
and before it reaches those who need it most,
What if it just…
Stops?

'The action or state of including or of being included.'

It seems simple, this dictionary definition of inclusion.
But it often causes confusion.

What does it actually mean?
Ensuring that everyone is a part of society?
That in every group of people, no one feels unseen?
The messages we receive
say that only one type of brain wiring is the 'right' one, it
    seems.
We've already started to challenge this,
as awareness spreads that this approach is missing something.

We make recommendations
to include the 'other' and to do this, we make *accommodations*.
I propose we pave a new way.
A more collaborative approach, for future generations.

I propose we see
Each other's Humanity.

Connecting human to human,
Without ruminating
on what sets us apart,
Paving a new way, with love at its heart.

With love as our guide, let's come together
And truly listen, to understand one another better.
Not to say *'this brain is wrong and that one is right'*
but to open a dialogue that will help us create spaces that
work for *every* neurotype.
Continuing as we are and just making exceptions
can lead to further isolation, and create even more rejection
for those who don't meet existing societal expectations.

So how do we create *real* inclusion?

By creating a society built on love,
where every individual knows that they are enough
just as they are.

A society founded in safety,
where we are all free
to explore our individual identities,
maintaining a sense of serenity
by remembering that

We are all one.

Only by returning repeatedly to this truth
can we create a truly inclusive community
That works for everybody.

So let's *all* throw our stones into the water, one by one
and create ripples
That can reach
Everyone.

Rachel B
reallyrachaelb.com

You can scan the code below to listen to Rachel B reading her poem:

References

Davis, T (2024) '5 tips for developing self-respect', *Psychology Today*, 18 July, URL: psychologytoday.com/us/blog/click-here-for-happiness/202312/5-tips-for-developing-self-respect

Fleming, L (2024) 'Agape love: The art of loving unconditionally: An ancient concept for modern relationships'. Verywell Mind, 7 March. URL: verywellmind.com/agape-love-8580332

Foerger, R H (2018) '"Become my son": A South African mother's response to the man who murdered both her son and her husband', International Forgiveness Institute, 24 June, URL: internationalforgiveness.com/2018/06/24/become-my-son-a-south-african-mothers-response-to-the-man-who-murdered-both-her-son-and-her-husband

Gupta, S (2022) 'The impact of self-respect on your life', Verywell Mind. URL: verywellmind.com/self-respect-importance-influences-and-strategies-for-improvement-6823525

Isaacs, W (1999) *Dialogue and the Art of Thinking Together*. Doubleday, pp 9, 11, 19, 21, 22, 110.

Kline, N (1999) *Time to Think: Listening to ignite the human mind*. Ward Lock, pp 27, 35, 36, 54, 58, 62, 67, 71, 74, 79, 84, 87.

Maister, D H, Green, C H & Galford, R M (2021) *The Trusted Advisor: 20th anniversary edition*. Free Press.

Mayes, A & Pinnock Fitts, S (2019) 'Coaching with identity in mind, the fifth domain | A model of coach inquiry, the ACTO Conference 2019'.

McLeod, S (2025) 'Maslow's hierarchy of needs', Simply Psychology, 14 March. URL: simplypsychology.org/maslow.html

Milton, D (2018) 'The double empathy problem'. National Autistic Society, 2 March. URL: autism.org.uk/advice-and-guidance/professional-practice/double-empathy

Neff, M A (2022) 'Spoon theory for autism and ADHD: The neurodivergent spoon drawer', Neurodivergent Insights. URL: neurodivergentinsights.com/the-neurodivergent-spoon-drawer-spoon-theory-for-adhders-and-autists

Newby, D & Nunez, L (2017) *The Unopened Gift*. Lightning Source UK.

Resilience Lab (2024) 'Agape love: How to love unconditionally',Resilience Lab, 5 December. URL: resiliencelab.us/thought-lab/agape-love-how-to-love-unconditionally

Rowland, L & Curry, O S (2018) 'A range of kindness activities boost happiness', *The Journal of Social Psychology* 159(3). URL: doi.org/10.1080/00224545.2018.1469461

Schwartz, R (2002) *The Skilled Facilitator*. Jossey-Bass.

Trzeciak, S, Mazzarelli, A & Seppälä, E (2023) 'Leading with compassion has research-backed benefits', *Harvard Business Review,* 27 February. URL: hbr.org/2023/02/leading-with-compassion-has-research-backed-benefits

van den Brink, J (2021) *The 3 Companions: Courage, Compassion & Wisdom: The powerful keys to happier work and a fulfilled life.* SRA Books.

About the author

Joan van den Brink is a management consultant, executive coach, coach supervisor and coach trainer. She believes that her life experiences and eclectic career have given her real insights into how to create environments where people can thrive. She is ardent about providing spaces in which individuals feel safe to be themselves and explore what lies beneath the surface so that they can better understand their actions and behaviours.

Joan graduated from the University of Cambridge with a PhD in Chemistry. She previously worked in marketing before moving into operations management. She became a management consultant specialising in leadership and organisational development, executive assessment and coaching in 2001, and led the HR and communications functions of a speciality chemicals company before setting up her own consultancy in 2014.

As an author, she engages with individuals who strongly connect with her chosen topics in mutually enriching conversations, which provide her with different perspectives and generate insights that inform her work. Her passion lies in supporting organisations to generate more inclusive environments.

Find out more about Joan's work at arabaconsulting.com.

EU Safety Representative: euComply OÜ Pärnu mnt 139b-14 11317 Tallinn
Estonia hello@eucompliancepartner.com +33 756 90241

www.ingramcontent.com/pod-product-compliance
Lightning Source LLC
Chambersburg PA
CBHW020534270326
41927CB00006B/563